S. Hrg. 115–184

RUSSIAN INFLUENCE AND UNCONVENTIONAL WARFARE OPERATIONS IN THE "GRAY ZONE": LESSONS FROM UKRAINE

HEARING

BEFORE THE

SUBCOMMITTEE ON EMERGING THREATS AND CAPABILITIES

OF THE

COMMITTEE ON ARMED SERVICES UNITED STATES SENATE

ONE HUNDRED FIFTEENTH CONGRESS

FIRST SESSION

———

MARCH 29, 2017

———

Printed for the use of the Committee on Armed Services

Available via the World Wide Web: http://www.fdsys.gov/

———

U.S. GOVERNMENT PUBLISHING OFFICE

28–945 PDF   WASHINGTON : 2018

CONTENTS

MARCH 29, 2017

(III)

RUSSIAN INFLUENCE AND UNCONVENTIONAL WARFARE OPERATIONS IN THE "GRAY ZONE": LESSONS FROM UKRAINE

WEDNESDAY, MARCH 29, 2017

U.S. SENATE,
SUBCOMMITTEE ON EMERGING
THREATS AND CAPABILITIES,
COMMITTEE ON ARMED SERVICES,
Washington, DC.

The subcommittee met, pursuant to notice, at 10:03 a.m. in Room SR–222, Russell Senate Office Building, Senator Joni Ernst (chairman of the subcommittee) presiding.

Subcommittee members present: Senators Ernst, Fischer, Sasse, Shaheen, Heinrich, and Peters.

OPENING STATEMENT OF SENATOR JONI ERNST

Senator ERNST. Good morning, everyone. We will call this meeting of the Subcommittee on Emerging Threats and Capabilities to order.

I want to thank the witnesses for being here today. This is a very important topic, and we are glad to have you and appreciate your point of view.

Today, the Emerging Threats and Capabilities Subcommittee meets to receive testimony on Russian influence and unconventional warfare operations in the "gray zone" and the lessons learned from those operations in Ukraine.

I would like to welcome our distinguished witnesses this morning: Dr. Olga Oliker, senior advisor and director of the Russia and Eurasia Program at the Center for Strategic and International Studies; Dr. Michael Carpenter, senior director of the Biden Center for Diplomacy and Global Engagement at the University of Pennsylvania; and retired Lieutenant General Charles Cleveland, former commander of U.S. Army Special Operations Command and currently a senior fellow at the Madison Policy Forum. Thank you very much for joining us today.

The invasion and illegal annexation of Crimea in the spring of 2014 represents the breadth of Russia's influence campaign in Ukraine and the violation of Ukrainian sovereignty represents the first attempt to change the boundary of a European nation since the end of the Cold War. Russian operations span the spectrum from covert information operations intended to influence political opinion to overt deployment of military forces for unconventional warfare designed to dominate civilian populations. We cannot afford to understate its importance or ignore its lessons. It is my hope our witnesses can help us understand in more detail what happened, why it was successful, and how to stop it from happening again in the future.

Last week, the commander of United States European Command [EUCOM], General Scaparrotti, characterized the Russian operations in Crimea as activities short of war or, as it is commonly referred to, the "gray zone." Russia's gray zone activities in Crimea are important for us to review today and unique because it was an influence campaign of propaganda and disinformation, culminating in the employment of Russian special operations forces on the sovereign territory of Ukraine.

This hearing today also allows us to discuss our own special operations forces. It is time we review their unconventional warfare capabilities.

I look forward to hearing from General Cleveland about his thoughts on the need to strengthen the capabilities in our special operations forces which may have understandably atrophied after over a decade focused on direct action counterterrorism missions.

The Russian influence campaign and unconventional warfare efforts in Ukraine contain all the hallmarks of the gray zone operations: ambiguity of attribution, indirect approach, and below the threshold of open conflict. As we continue to see Russia conduct these operations across the globe, I hope our witnesses today can better help us understand and better counter these efforts.

Senator Heinrich, would you like an opening statement?

STATEMENT OF SENATOR MARTIN HEINRICH

Senator HEINRICH. Thank you, Chairwoman Ernst. I want to thank you for holding this important hearing and thank our witnesses for their testimony on Russia's use of influence activities and unconventional warfare in the so-called gray zone that encompasses the struggle between nations and other non-state actors short of direct military conflict.

This hearing builds on the testimony the full committee received last week on the security situation in Europe. At last Thursday's hearing, General Scaparrotti, commander of United States European Command, stated that Russia is using a range of military and nonmilitary tools to, "undermine the international system and discredit those in the West who have created it".

When I asked him about Russia's conduct of denial, deception, and disinformation operations, General Scaparrotti stressed that Russia takes not only a military approach but a, "whole-of-government approach" to information warfare to include intelligence and other groups, which accounts for its rapid and agile use of social media and cyber.

Russia's use of the full range of political, economic, and informational tools at its disposal provides it the means to influence operations in the gray zone short of a direct conventional war. Today's hearing is an opportunity to examine the lessons drawn from Russia's maligned activities in the Ukraine.

In 2014, General Scaparrotti's predecessor at EUCOM Commander General Breedlove said that Russia was engaged in, "the most amazing information warfare blitzkrieg we have ever seen in the history of information warfare". Russia used information warfare as a dimension of its own military operations in Ukraine, including the sowing of confusion and disorganization prior to initiating more traditional military operations.

Russia's combination of information warfare with other unconventional warfare techniques, including the training, equipping, and advising of proxies and funding of separatist groups, is what allowed them to, "change the facts on the ground" before the international community could respond effectively through traditional means.

This is relevant not simply as a history lesson but to better prepare us for the kinds of operations we can expect to see Russia conduct in the future. For example, the January 2017 intelligence community assessment on Russian activities and intentions in the 2016 United States presidential election assessed that what occurred last year represents a significant escalation in Russia's influence operations that is likely to continue here in the United States, as well as elsewhere.

So there is much to explore with our witnesses this morning, and again, I thank them and look forward to their testimony.

Senator ERNST. Thank you, Ranking Member. We will start with Dr. Oliker, please.

STATEMENT OF OLGA OLIKER, SENIOR ADVISOR AND DIRECTOR, RUSSIA AND EURASIA PROGRAM, CENTER FOR STRATEGIC AND INTERNATIONAL STUDIES

Dr. OLIKER. Thank you very much, Chairwoman Ernst, Ranking Member Heinrich, members of the subcommittee. I am honored to be here today. So I have been asked to address the topic of Russian influence and unconventional warfare operations in the gray zone, lessons from Ukraine. I will talk briefly about what we saw in Ukraine, a little bit about Russian activities elsewhere, and then I will talk about how the Russians appear to think about these issues. I will conclude with some thoughts about what that means for all of us.

Really quick, a definitional point as it were. We are talking—when we talk about the gray zone, we are talking in this case about operations that are not clearly peace or war and perhaps intentionally meant to blur the line between the two. A note of caution is that these lines are always a bit blurry. When Carl von Clausewitz wrote that war is an extension of politics, he did not mean the politics ends when war begins. Rather, we should expect military, political, economic, and diplomatic instruments to be brought to bear to attain national goals, together and separately.

But when we talk about the two things I think we are going to focus on here today, military actions characterized by subterfuge and efforts to mask who is and who is not a combatant and information operations, we have a different—we face a bit of a different challenge. One of these, information influence operations, clearly on the noncombat side of the equation. On the other hand, subterfuge and efforts to mask who is and who is not a combatant are something that the Russians have been exercising increasingly and increasingly effectively. I think we want to think about both of these less in terms of whether they are or are not gray zone and more in terms of their strategic effects.

So turning to Ukraine, in terms of the public information campaign, Russian language print, internet, and television media had pretty heavy saturation in Ukraine long before 2014 and particularly in Crimea and in the east. They propagated a narrative in 2013 in the lead up to the expected EU [European Union] Association signature that was meant to convince audiences that EU Association would lead to political chaos and economic collapse of Ukraine, and social media activism amplified these messages.

As time went on and as unrest grew, the message came to include attacks on the protesters on Ukraine's Maidan Nezalezhnosti, Independence Square. They attacked the government that took control after Yanukovych fled the country. They attacked Western governments, which were depicted as orchestrating what was termed a fascist coup. Eventually, of course, they attacked the elected government of President Petro Poroshenko.

Now, these messages probably resonated most with people already inclined to believe them, people who were nervous about EU Association and distrustful of the West. That was a lot of folks in both Crimea and east Ukraine. So Russian information operations I would argue may have helped bring some of those people into the streets, implemented some of the unrest, but I would also point out that it is important to remember that is not how Russian annexed Crimea. This, while almost bloodless, was a military operation made possible in large part by Russia's preexisting preponderance of force on the peninsula. I would also say that information influence operations of this sort were not responsible for keeping the conflict in east Ukraine going. That also took Russian military support and eventually Russian troops.

Another form of influence that I would like to talk about in Ukraine is that engendered by economic and political ties. Ukraine's and Russia's economies were deeply intertwined since the collapse of the Soviet Union. Some of this was corrupt, including with the Yanukovych regime and its supporters. Some of it was not. I would argue that corrupt ties, just like the rest of the corruption in Ukraine, creates a lobby and created a lobby against EU Association, which was going to bring with it requirements of greater transparency and more open business climates. But the broad range of economic relationships, many of them completely legal, also worried Ukrainians who thought that their livelihoods were genuinely less certain if ties with Russia waned. Many of those people were in Ukraine's east and south.

On the military side, of course the most touted example of Russian unconventional operations is the insertion of additional forces into Crimea in late February of 2014. Wearing uniforms without insignia, these personnel, which we termed little green men and the Russians termed polite people, pretended to be Ukrainian soldiers and police. They seized the Parliament building. They surrounded an airbase. The lack of uniform markings contributed to confusion, and enabled Russia to deny their deployment of additional forces to Crimea.

Similarly, Russia has denied its support for separatists in eastern Ukraine, as well as the insertion of its regular army troops into that fight as both advisors and active forces. As with Crimea, this feeds confusion and allows for deniability. The actual fighting in east Ukraine though is very conventional, tending towards a great deal of artillery and some trench warfare.

Cyber tools have been used by Russia but with limited effect. The most interesting exception is the December 2015 attack on Ukraine's power grid, which took down electricity to hundreds of thousands of people for several hours. So that is interesting because it is using cyber tools for the sorts of effects you might normally use military forces for. But again, the effect in this particular case was not that great.

So turning outside Ukraine, we see influence operations in full swing in Europe and even here in the United States, and I am not sure I would actually call those gray zone, but I would call them efforts to undermine and subvert Western unity and trust in existing governments and institutions, so I do think there are important.

So in some ways what Russia does elsewhere is similar to what it does in Ukraine. Russian language media targets Russian-speaking populations around the world, particularly in neighboring countries where the media is often popular. Russia also supports outlets around the world such as *RT* [Russia Today] and *Sputnik,* which broadcasts in other languages, including English. The M.O. [Modus Operandi] of these outlets is to raise questions about the reporting of other sources and of other government statements and views such as by denying Russian military presence in Ukraine. They also tend to highlight what they portray as the hypocrisy of these non-Russian governments, for instance, collateral damage caused by United States and NATO military actions. These messages are then amplified by social media, including through so-called trolls.

Happily, there is no evidence to date that these messages are reaching audiences previously unfavorable to them and changing minds. Just like in Ukraine where Russian messages were most effective with those predisposed to trust them, the same is true around the world. I would argue that the real threat posed by these phenomena is less their independent effect but the fact that they fall into an echo chamber. They are one sliver of a much larger increase in chaos and untruth in the information space as a whole.

The widespread use of these same techniques of smears, blatant lies, uncorroborated reporting, amplified by like-minded social media users, real and robotic, created an environment in which it is indeed really hard to tell truth from falsehood. The resulting situation is not so much one in which more people trust Russian sources but one in which people only trust whichever sources they prefer and discount all the others. This is dangerous. Russia is exploiting it, but we make a mistake if we look at it as uniquely or predominantly a Russian threat.

I also want to talk a little bit about Russian economic influence in Europe and elsewhere. Here, too, it is a bit of a mixed bag. Countries where there are strong business ties to Russia do indeed tend to have lobbies that support closer ties at the national level. This is not necessarily nefarious, right? It becomes nefarious when we see efforts on the part of the Russian Government to leverage it into something that increases Russian influence in ways that are not for the good of both countries.

A greater concern might be Russian support for fringe parties in Europe. We see these ties in Hungary, in France, in Austria, among others. We do see that leaders and members of right-wing and ultranationalist parties throughout the West have looked to Russia as a model, and we have seen that the Kremlin increasingly looks at these groups and supporting them because they tend to be anti-EU and sometimes anti-NATO as a mechanism for weakening Western unity. Russia, I would argue, might be particularly emboldened by what looks like recent success on this front, though I would also point out that the Kremlin is increasingly very nervous about its own right-wing nationalists and has been cracking down on them. So that is something to keep in mind.

So in the United States of course our intelligence agencies have judged that Russia was trying to influence our election last year. There is nothing unusual, I would say, about using cyber tools to collect intelligence. It is unusual and crosses any number of lines to then take action to use the information collected that way to interfere in other countries' political processes. It is likely to me that Russia's expectations were that they could disrupt the United States election, contributing to confusion and raising questions about its legitimacy.

If they believe this has been successful and even more so if they judge that they had a hand in the outcome, something I personally do not believe to be the case, they may be emboldened to undertake similar actions elsewhere and also in the United States again. We see evidence of this in Europe. This said, I would underline the fact that Russian efforts exploit weaknesses already in place rather than creating them.

So what do the Russians think about all this? The Russians are writing a lot about the broad range of mechanisms that can advance national and political goals. What is interesting is that they write about them not as approaches Russia can use but rather as tools that are being developed by the West against Russia, and they cite everything from economic sanctions to their longstanding complaint about supportive what they call colour revolutions. They view this as a concerted whole-of-government effort to weaken and overthrow governments abroad and that Russia has to learn how to counter these.

They assume a substantial Western advantage in all of these areas, and importantly, Russian writing on the future of war also tends to emphasize the importance of conventional warfare and particularly air power and advanced technologies. So I think this is a very interesting thing to keep in mind. Their argument is that we do this to them, and when they write about the things that they see in the American literature, they completely ignore the references to Russia undertaking these actions.

So, bottom line, I think there is no question that Russia is undertaking action across the spectrum of political, diplomatic, and military power. I would warn against viewing Russian approaches as a well-thought-out strategy throughout the world. Russia is testing approaches, it is experimenting, and it is trying to build on successes. So I would say one of the most important lessons for us to take from Russia's action in Ukraine and elsewhere is that Russia is learning lessons. It is studying what works and what does not. It is assessing how to adapt these techniques.

So take Crimea and east Ukraine. The Crimea operation was extremely successful. Russian planners then thought something similar could succeed in eastern Ukraine and perhaps Ukraine as a whole. They were proven wrong. They adapted, they recalibrated, they changed their approach. So this is one of many reasons that I do not think a Crimea-like scenario is what we should be worrying about in, say, Estonia or elsewhere in the Baltics.

Russia's ability to use military personnel without insignia while denying their presence was not just specific to the Ukrainian situation. It was also not decisive in the success or failure of Russian efforts. Russia's success rather was based on the combination of large-scale military presence and a Crimea population that was confused and sympathetic. This way, the insertion of the personnel without insignia could be helpful, and all of this, we must remember, worked far less well in east Ukraine with a more skeptical population and failed entirely elsewhere such as in Odessa.

So not only is there excellent reason to think that the population of, say, Narva and Estonia, which a lot of us think about a lot, has more in common with Odessa than Donetsk or Sevastopol, but I would also point out that Estonians are at this point hyperaware of this particular threat and the Russians know that and they know all of this and they know all of these lessons. So should Russia have designs on the Baltics, they may try many things, but I would be surprised if the operation looked much like anything we saw in Ukraine.

One question I am asking myself today is whether there is a Crimea equivalent in the influence operation space. Is there a point at which Russia feels it has hit upon a successful tactic but it overreaches? I believe that its efforts to affect election campaigns may get them to that point, but Russia's limitations in its efforts to weaken existing institutions depend tremendously on the strength of those institutions. Russian tools exploit weaknesses. The challenge then is to eliminate or at least mitigate those weaknesses.

I will close there. I thank you, and I look forward to your questions.

[The prepared statement of Dr. Oliker follows:]

PREPARED STATEMENT BY DR. OLGA OLIKER

Subcommittee Chair Ernst, Ranking Member Heinrich, and members of the subcommittee, I am honored to be here today. I have been asked to address the topic of Russian influence and unconventional warfare operations in the "gray zone:" lessons from Ukraine. I begin by defining terms a bit, because there are a few ways to think about this question. I will then talk briefly about what we have seen in Ukraine, Russian activities elsewhere, and how Russians appear to think about these issues, before concluding with some thoughts about what we in the United States might learn from these experiences.

DEFINING TERMINOLOGY

The "gray zone" means different things to different people. In the United States in recent years, one definition that has emerged is geographical. It refers to countries and parts of the world to which there is not a clear United States commitment, but where the United States has interests. In Europe, this means countries that are not members of NATO (as NATO members do have an explicit security commitment from the United States). This, of course, includes Ukraine.

Another definition for gray zone refers to operations, specifically those that are more difficult to define as either peace or war, and indeed possibly those undertaken intentionally to obfuscate and blur the lines between the two. Of course, those lines have always been blurry. Carl von Clausewitz wrote that war is an extension of politics; he did not mean that politics ends when war begins, or that there is a stark divide between the two. Rather, military, political, economic, and diplomatic instruments should all be expected to be used to attain national goals, together and separately. Armed conflict then, is, definitionally enough, characterized by the use of armaments in a conflict, almost certainly alongside other tools.

In the context of Russian operations in Ukraine, we are interested today in two kinds of activities. Influence operations, which seek to leverage media and propaganda efforts as well as business and political ties to attain national goals are, if not always aboveboard, surely short of armed conflict. They thus may be in the gray zone from a geographical perspective, but are not from an operational perspective. This said, such actions, even when undertaken in countries that are not in the "gray zone," may still be of strategic interest. Unconventional warfare, if it is unquestionably armed action by military personnel, is of course armed conflict. If, however, it is characterized by subterfuge and actions by those who cannot be clearly identified as combatants, it may be in the operational gray zone as well (it is also, in its own way, an influence operation, in that it seeks to affect the calculus of other parties). In Ukraine, we see all of these to varying degrees, with a range of implications for other parts of Europe and the rest of the world.

INFLUENCE OPERATIONS IN UKRAINE

As I alluded to above, I see two types of non-military influence operations that have been and continue to be used by the Russian Federation in Ukraine and elsewhere. The first is public information campaigns and propaganda—efforts to target a broad population with press stories, social media tools, and so forth. The second is building up and leveraging business and political relationships. This includes support to political activists and parties, and efforts to develop business "lobbies" that will support Russian goals.

I start with the first of these. In Ukraine, Russian-language print, internet, and television media had fairly heavy saturation prior to 2014, particularly in Crimea and in the East. Their narrative, aimed at both Russians and Ukrainians, was meant to convince audiences that EU association would lead to political chaos, widespread homosexuality, and economic collapse. Social media activism amplified these messages, particularly on Russian-language websites. As the crisis unfolded, the coverage denigrated the protesters on Ukraine's Maidan Nezalezhnosti (Independence Square) who called for the ouster of then-President Yanukovych; the government that took control after Yanukovych fled; Western governments, which were depicted as orchestrating this "fascist coup;" and eventually the elected government of new President Petro Poroshenko. Social media disseminated both intercepted and apparently doctored recordings of Western officials discussing the situation in Ukraine, with the intent to both embarrass and to suggest a Western hand behind Kyiv's emerging government. The narrative emphasized unrest in Kyiv and elsewhere and reported that fascist gangs were roaming the capital city's streets. Another thread sought to instill and play on fear among Russian-speaking Ukrainians that they would be persecuted by the new government (this was admittedly helped along by some of the rhetoric in Kyiv, including an ill-considered, and quickly reversed, effort to require the use of Russian in official transactions when other languages had previously been allowed).

What did this do? I would argue that it likely did make some people even more nervous than they had been before. But the extent to which Russian media coverage contributed to protests and unrest in both Crimea and Eastern Ukraine is difficult to judge. These campaigns were surely most successful with populations that were already inclined to believe them—people who were nervous about EU association, distrustful of the West, and, once a new government took shape in Kyiv, fearful of what this might mean. In Crimea, where a large part of the self-identified ethnic Russian majority is comprised by retired Russian military personnel and their families, and where the Russian Black Sea Fleet continued to be based after the collapse of the USSR, this was a substantial proportion of the population. In Eastern Ukraine, where Yanukovych had his base of support, this message also resonated. But if information operations of this sort helped bring people into the streets, they cannot be credited with Russia's annexation of Crimea. This, while almost bloodless, was a military action made possible in large part by Russia's pre-existing preponderance of force on the peninsula.

Similarly, while Russian propaganda may well have played a role in public dissatisfaction, to truly get a conflict going in Eastern Ukraine took more than that. As the protests grew, there was increasing evidence that while some of the protesters were local, Russians crossed the border to join in as well. When fighting flared, Russian supplies of armaments (and, it soon became clear, advisers and troops) were what kept it viable in the face of Ukrainian response. Today, Russian efforts to propagandize to Ukrainian populations in the East are blocked and countered, to the extent possible, by the Ukrainian government. However, the best defense against false narratives at this point is surely the stream of displaced persons from the separatist-controlled territories, the experience of continued fighting for those near the front lines, and other first-and second-hand knowledge of the realities of the situation.

Influence engendered by economic and political ties presents a different dynamic. Ukraine's and Russia's economies were deeply intertwined since the collapse of the USSR. This involved both legal, above-board activity and a variety of corrupt contacts and ties, including with the Yanukovych regime and its supporters. Ukraine's East and South were particularly closely tied to Russia, with highly interdependent economies. To the extent that these ties and exchanges were corrupt, they, along with other forms of corruption, made it highly unlikely that their beneficiaries would support EU association, with its requirements of greater transparency and a more open business climate as a whole. Today, it is plausible to argue that some continuing ties with Russia, many of them increasingly secretive, may be part of what is hampering reform efforts and thus undermining Ukraine's future. But the broad range of economic relationships, most of them completely legal, also created concerns among the many Ukrainians whose livelihoods were genuinely less certain if ties with Russia waned, something that surely exacerbated their other fears.

UNCONVENTIONAL MILITARY OPERATIONS IN UKRAINE

The line between conventional and unconventional military operations is not always a clear one. Among unconventional operations are counterinsurgency and insurgency missions, the use of specialized forces, electronic warfare and cyber campaigns, and such things as the use and backing of foreign government and non-government forces as proxies. All of this is present in most conflicts, to varying extents. Because of our focus on the "gray zone," we are most interested here in areas that appear to be, genuinely or arguably, short of actual international armed conflict.

In the case of Russian operations in Ukraine, perhaps the most touted example is the insertion of additional Russian forces into Crimea in late February 2014.[1] Wearing uniforms without insignia, these personnel, termed "little green men" in the Ukrainian and Western press and "polite people" by Russia, took an active part in events on the peninsula, including seizing the Parliament building and surrounding the Belbek air base. Russian military personnel also pretended to be Ukrainian military and police and worked with local "self-defense" units. Their ack of uniform markings contributed to confusion, even as Russia denied the deployment of additional forces to Crimea.

Russia has also denied its support for the separatists fighting the Ukrainian Army in Eastern and Southern Ukraine, as well as the insertion of its regular army troops into that fight as both advisors and active troops. Here, too, we see examples of Russian forces masquerading as locals. We also, of course, see the support and development of a proxy force. As with the "little green men" in Crimea, this feeds confusion and allows for deniability. The actual fighting in Eastern Ukraine, however, is highly conventional, tending towards a great deal of artillery and some trench warfare.

Finally, it is important to note the use of cyber in the Ukraine conflict. Early in the conflict, these took the form of distributed denial of service (DDOS) and defacement attacks on Ukrainian government and NATO websites. This was more a form of harassment, however, than anything else. More debilitating was a December 2015 attack on Ukraine's power grid, which shut down electricity to hundreds of thousands of people for several hours. Both Ukrainian and United States officials blamed Moscow. If this was, indeed, an orchestrated attack by Russia, it is an example of precisely the type of cyber operation that could be seen as warfare, in that it approximates effects similar to those that might be attained through the use of armed force.

---

[1] Russia of course had a sizable pre-existing military presence on the peninsula, in the form of its Black Sea Fleet.

RUSSIAN ACTIVITIES ELSEWHERE

In assessing Russian activities outside of Ukraine, I focus on influence operations. In the military context, the only current example of Russian operations outside of Ukraine is Syria, where the most unconventional aspect is Russian support of proxy forces, which the United States and its allies are also engaged in. As noted above, influence operations against the United States and its NATO allies cannot really be termed "gray zone" operations, because they fit neither the geographical nor operational definition of the term. However, the growing concern about these activities requires us to pay attention to them as what they are—political influence operations undertaken with hostile intent, in this case, efforts to undermine and subvert Western unity and trust in existing governments and institutions.

Russian influence campaigns outside of Ukraine share some similarities with its activities within that country. In terms of media and social media efforts, one aspect of this is Russian-language media targeting Russian populations around the world, and particularly in neighboring countries, where it is often popular. In addition, much attention has been paid in recent years to, on the one hand, Russian government-supported outlets around the world, such as RT and Sputnik, which are heavily advertised and, by broadcasting and publishing in English and other languages, able to reach a wide population around the world. While these outlets do consistently report Russian government positions, they are probably more effective when they raise questions about the reporting of other sources, and of other government statements and views—such as by denying Russian military presence in Ukraine. They also tend to highlight what they portray as the hypocrisy of non-Russian governments, for instance by highlighting collateral damage caused by United States and NATO military actions abroad.

Also notable is the Kremlin's use of social media outlets. This was also evident in Ukraine, and is utilized much the same way around the world, in a range of languages. Researchers have unearthed so-called "troll farms" that rely on human-and machine-run social media accounts to amplify Kremlin messages and raise doubts about other viewpoints. This, like the direct media campaigns, tends to combine elements of truth and falsehood, building trust among like-minded people on a range of issues in order to heighten tension and frustration and perhaps further expand influence on other issues.

While we can establish the presence of a sizeable Russian effort in this regard, this begs the most important question: does any of this work? Happily, there is no evidence to date that these messages are reaching audiences previously unfavorable to them and changing minds. In Ukraine, Russian media messages were most effective with those predisposed to trust them. The same is true of both Russian and foreign-language media and social media efforts elsewhere in the world. I would argue that the real threat posed by these phenomena is not their independent effect, but the fact that they are just one sliver of a much larger increase in chaos and untruth in the information space. The widespread use of these same techniques of smears, blatant lies, and uncorroborated reporting amplified by like-minded social media users (paid, robotic, and genuine) create an environment in which it is, indeed, difficult to tell truth from falsehood. The resulting environment is not so much one in which more people trust Russian sources, but in which people only trust whatever sources they prefer, and discount all others. This is dangerous, and Russia is exploiting the situation, but it is far from a uniquely, or predominantly, Russian threat.

Russian economic influence in Europe and elsewhere is a mixed bag. It is true that there are pro-Russian politicians in Europe, and that some of them have ties to Russian business. But it can be hard to figure out which of these came first. For instance, when Hungary's Prime Minister Viktor Orban supports collaboration with Russian firms, is this because he seeks closer relations with Moscow (which he does) or does he seek closer relations with Moscow because of the economic gains that would accrue? In the United States, firms that had business in Russia have been more skeptical of sanctions; this plays out similarly in Europe. France's Republican Party also supports a better relationship with Russia, no doubt in part because it has constituents in industries such as defense, energy, luxury goods, transportation, and banking, all of which stand to gain from more trade with Russia. Many years of solid economic ties between Russia and Germany lead some German parties to also desire better relations with Moscow. The fact is that most of the economic ties that exist are surely above-board, the product of years of seeking to integrate Russia into the global economy. Moreover, the requirements of operating in the West force Russian companies to adopt higher standards for transparency, which may have positive longer-term effects. Thus, while any Kremlin efforts to leverage economic ties for political gain should be monitored, this does not mean that business with Russian firms and individuals should be demonized.

A greater concern may be Russia's support for fringe parties in Europe. Bela Kovacs, who helped finance Hungary's pro-Russian ultranationalist Jobbik party, may have used Russian funds to do so. He is now under investigation for spying for Russia. Not a few have noticed the 2014 and 2016 loans from the First Czech Russian Bank to France's far right National Front Party—to say nothing of party leader Marine Le Pen's friendly relationship with Vladimir Putin. Late in 2016, Austria's far-right Freedom Party inked a cooperation deal with the United Russia Party. There is no doubt that leaders and members of right wing and nationalist parties throughout the West see Russia as a model. It is equally clear that the Kremlin sees support for these political groups, which tend to be anti-EU and sometimes anti-NATO as well, as a means of weakening Western unity. It may be particularly emboldened by seeming recent successes. Interestingly, the Kremlin is increasingly wary of its own right wing nationalists, and has been cracking down on them.

In the United States, of course, our intelligence agencies have judged that Russia released information obtained through cyberhacks of American organizations, including political party organizations, in order to influence our Presidential election last year. There is nothing particularly unusual about using cyber tools to collect intelligence. It is unusual, and crosses any number of lines, to then take action to use such information to interfere in another country's political processes. It is likely that Russia's expectations of influence were that they could, in this way, disrupt the United States election, contributing to confusion and raising questions about legitimacy. If they believe that this has been a success, and even more so if they judge that they had a hand in the outcome (something I do not believe to be the case), they may be emboldened to undertake similar actions in the future, vis-á-vis the United States and other countries. We have certainly heard rumors that such efforts are underway in the context of Germany's election, upcoming in September of this year. Again, particularly in concert with Russian support of right wing parties in Europe, this should be watched carefully. However, I would underline that Russian efforts at best exploit weaknesses already in place. It seems highly unlikely that they can be decisive under current conditions.

RUSSIAN DOCTRINE AND THINKING

Before turning to the lessons we might draw from all of this, it is worth stopping to ask how Russian military and security analysts view the situation. While much recent Russian analysis of modern-day conflict and warfare highlights the broad range of mechanisms that can advance political goals, Russian analysts tend to present these not as approaches Russia can use, but rather as tools that are being developed by the West against Russia, which Russia must learn to counter. This was evident in Russia's most recent military doctrine, released in late 2014,[2] and in a variety of analysis and writing produced since. Even Russian discussions of so-called "hybrid" conflict, a term that they have picked up from Western authors, ignore the fact that those analysts use the term almost exclusively to describe Russian political and military action. Russians, by contrast, use it to describe a range of Western activity, from economic sanctions to support of "color revolutions," all geared to weaken and overthrow governments abroad. Moreover, they assume a substantial Western advantage in these areas.[3] This was the nature of the much touted 2013 piece by Russian General Staff Chief Valery Gerasimov, which was, in the aftermath of Crimea, read by many in the West as presenting a new Russian approach to warfare. In fact, the text described a Russian view of Western approaches.[4]

Despite these concerns, Russian writing on the future of war continues also to emphasize the importance of conventional warfare, with particular emphasis on air power and advanced technologies. The most recent piece by Gerasimov, published

---

[2] Vladimir Putin, "The Military Doctrine of the Russian Federation," December 25, 2014. English language version available at *http://rusemb.org.uk/press/2029* (accessed March 27, 2017)

[3] Ibid. See also Samuel Charap, "The Ghost of Hybrid War." Survival (00396338) 57, no. 6 (December 2015): 51–58. For more recent examples, see Valerii' Gerasimov, "Mir Na Graniakh Voiny," March 15, 2017; S. G. Chekinov and S. A. Bogdanov, "E'voliutsiia Sushchnosti I Soderzhaniia Poniatiia 'voi'na' v XXI Stoletii," January 2017; V. A. Kiselev, "K Kakim Voi'nam Neobkhodimo Gotovit' Vooruzhennye Sily Rossii," March 2017.

[4] Valerii' Gerasimov, "Tsennost' Nauki V Predvidenii," February 27, 2013; Charap, "The Ghost of Hybrid War"; Charles K. Bartles, "Getting Gerasimov Right," Military Review 96, no. 1 (February 1, 2016): 30–38.

just a few weeks ago, argues strongly that for all the new and creative ways Western countries are seeking to subvert Russia, conventional capabilities are at the core of what the country should itself emphasize.[5]

WHAT WE SHOULD BE LEARNING FROM UKRAINE AND ELSEWHERE

There is no question that Russia is undertaking action across the spectrum of political, diplomatic, and military power. However, I warn against viewing Russian approaches as a well thought out strategy undertaken throughout the world. As is evidenced by Russian writing on these topics, Russia is testing approaches, experimenting, and trying to build on successes. Thus, one of the most important lessons from Russian actions in Ukraine and elsewhere in the world is that Russia is learning lessons from its own operations. It is carefully studying what works and what doesn't, and trying to assess how to adapt techniques for other purposes. Take the example of Crimea and East Ukraine. The Crimea operation was extremely successful. At least partly on its basis, Russian planners thought that something similar could succeed in Eastern Ukraine, and perhaps Ukraine as a whole. They were quickly proven wrong, and they recalibrated their goals and their tactics accordingly.

This is one of the many reasons that I do not think that a Crimea-like scenario is what we should be worrying about in, for example, Estonia or elsewhere in the Baltics. Russia's ability to use military personnel without insignia while denying their presence was specific to the Ukrainian situation, and not, in the end, decisive in the success or failure of Russian efforts. These and other Russian tactics of supporting separatist attacks on government buildings, backed by propaganda and influence operations, worked best where there was large-scale military presence and the population was confused and generally sympathetic—that is to say, in Crimea. It worked far less well where the population was more skeptical as in Eastern Ukraine, and such approaches proved completely ineffective where Russia did not have much influence, for instance in Odessa. Not only is there excellent reason to think that the population of Narva, in Estonia, has more in common with Odessa than Donetsk, much less Sevastopol, but authorities are at this point hyper-aware of this particular threat, and the Russians know that. Should Russia have designs on the Baltics, they may try many things, but I would be surprised if the operation looked much like Ukraine.

One question I am asking myself today is whether there is a Crimea equivalent in the influence operations space. Is there a point at which Russia feels that it has hit upon a successful tactic and it overreaches? I believe that its efforts to affect election campaigns may play just that role. But Russia's limitations in its efforts to weaken existing institutions depend tremendously on the strength of those institutions. Russian tools exploit weaknesses. The challenge, then, is to eliminate, or at least mitigate, those weaknesses. Thank you and I look forward to your questions.

Senator ERNST. Thank you very much, Dr. Oliker.
Dr. Carpenter?

STATEMENT OF MICHAEL R. CARPENTER, SENIOR DIRECTOR, BIDEN CENTER FOR DIPLOMACY AND GLOBAL ENGAGEMENT, UNIVERSITY OF PENNSYLVANIA

Dr. CARPENTER. Chairman Ernst, Ranking Member Heinrich, members of the subcommittee, thank you for this opportunity to speak about the lessons learned from Russia's influence operations in Ukraine.

Russia's unconventional war in Ukraine has demonstrated a formidable toolkit of measures for fighting in the gray zone from world-class cyber and electronic warfare capabilities to sophisticated covert action and disinformation campaigns. Russia has used propaganda, sabotage, assassination, bribery, proxy fronts, and false-flag operations to supplement its considerable conventional forces in eastern Ukraine.

---

[5] Gerasimov, "Mir Na Graniakh Voiny."

Moscow has been doing its homework. Recognizing its conventional capabilities lag behind NATO's, Russia has been investing in asymmetric capabilities to gain advantage over conventionally superior Western militaries. At the same time, Moscow has dispensed with its longstanding foreign policy of cooperating with the West where possible and competing where necessary and now seeks to actively undermine the transatlantic alliance and delegitimize the international order through a continuous and sustained competition short of conflict.

But even with Russia's well-honed unconventional capabilities, the United States and its NATO allies can prevail in this competition if we recognize the Kremlin's goals for what they are, develop smart strategies to counter them, properly align our institutional structures, and invest in the right capabilities.

Today, I would like to briefly highlight six areas where the United States must counter Russia's new generation warfare. First is information warfare. In eastern Ukraine and Russia, the Kremlin has used its monopoly on broadcast television in particular to spread false narratives. For example, as Olga mentioned, that fascists control the government in Kyiv. Here in the United States, these lies are easily debunked, but we should not underestimate how even here Russian trolls and bots can spam us with propaganda and thereby shift the media's focus from one story to another.

I believe an independent commission should be established to identify and take action against Russian misinformation in addition to resourcing a more robust interagency body. Frankly, we should also go beyond debunking lies in the Western media space and take a much more active role in exposing corruption and repression inside Russia.

Second, we urgently need to upgrade our cyber defenses and those of our allies and partners. Regulatory oversight should be strengthened to ensure that private corporations that manage much of our critical infrastructure are taking the necessary steps to harden defenses. I also support the establishment of a national cyber academy and expanding the Pentagon's public-private partnerships with the IT [information technology] sector.

In cases where the United States is able to attribute a specific attack, our response must be firm, timely, and proportionate. The [persona non grata] PNG-ing of Russian officials in response to Russia's cyber attack is unfortunately just a symbolic act with very few real consequences. Until our adversaries learn that the cost of such actions outweigh the consequences, they will keep probing.

Third, we must get better in exposing Russia's covert operations. In addition to its little green men, as Olga referred to, Russia also deployed what SNMs call little gray men who organize demonstrations and seize government buildings across eastern Ukraine in the spring of 2014. The lesson we learn here is that once these forces were outed in Ukraine, strong social resilience and effective local law enforcement succeeded in thwarting most efforts to foment insurgency. Where Russia's efforts succeeded in Ukraine it was largely because they were backed by coercion and more overt military force, a point you made as well.

Fourth, Russia relies on a range of proxy groups to carry out subversive actions. However, Moscow's greatest success with proxy forces has not been on the battlefield but rather on the diplomatic stage. One of the biggest mistakes made by Western leaders of the so-called Normandy Group was to elevate the role of Russian proxies in the February 2015 Minsk Agreement. The result today is a kabuki negotiation in which Russia's proxies stonewall any meaningful progress on implementing Minsk, and Russia largely avoids blame.

Fifth, sabotage and terrorism have been used to great effect in the Ukraine conflict. A week ago today, former Duma member Denis Voronenkov was assassinated in central Kyiv on the same day as an act of sabotage destroyed a munitions depot. As with proxies, preventing terrorism and sabotage depends on good intelligence and strong social resilience. Ukraine has in fact averted many terrorist incidents over the last three years thanks to tipoffs from vigilant citizens and good law enforcement work.

Sixth, Russia has dramatically ramped up its political influence operations not just in Ukraine but throughout Europe and the United States. To counteract Russian influence operations, we need more transparency in political party financing, more effective anticorruption tools, better sharing of information on financial crimes, and stronger law enforcement to root out entrenched and corrosive Russian patronage networks.

I believe the United States should establish a standing interagency operational body dedicated solely to interdicting Russian influence operations. Most importantly, however, it is absolutely vital that an independent special prosecutor be appointed in the United States to investigate allegations of ties between the Russian Government and United States political actors during the last election cycle. This is the one Russian influence operation that most directly affects our national security, and to protect the integrity of our democratic institutions, we simply must follow the evidence where it leads, free from political influence.

Finally, if I may be permitted to say a few words on how the United States should push back on Russia's unconventional war in Ukraine itself, I believe we should start by expanding our military training programs and by providing Ukraine with much-needed defensive weapons. On the diplomatic front, the United States must stop outsourcing the negotiations to France and Germany and get directly involved to help the parties develop a roadmap for implementing the Minsk Agreement. This roadmap must specify dates by which actions must be completed and consequences for failing to meet these deadlines.

To sharpen United States leverage, we should consider unilaterally tightening financial sanctions if Russia fails to meet these benchmarks. Lastly, the United States needs to continue to support Ukraine's reforms in part by applying strict conditionality to United States assistance but also by encouraging our European partners to play a much more active role than they have today.

Chairman Ernst, Ranking Member Heinrich, subcommittee members, Russia's operations in the gray zone have not only grown bolder in the last decade, but they have expanded from states on Russia's periphery like Georgia and Ukraine to Europe and even to the United States. Our responses at home and abroad must demonstrate the seriousness and urgency that these threats demand. Thank you, and I look forward to taking your questions.

[The prepared statement of Dr. Carpenter follows:]

PREPARED STATEMENT BY DR. MICHAEL CARPENTER

Note: The statements, views, and policy recommendations expressed in this testimony reflect the opinions of the author alone, and do not necessarily reflect the positions of the Biden Center for Diplomacy and Global Engagement or the University of Pennsylvania.

Chairman Ernst, Ranking Member Heinrich, members of the Subcommittee on Emerging Threats and Capabilities, thank you for the opportunity to speak about the lessons learned from Russian influence operations in Ukraine.

Russia's unconventional war against Ukraine has revealed a formidable toolkit of measures for fighting in the so-called "gray zone," from world-class cyber and electronic warfare capabilities to sophisticated covert action and disinformation operations. Russia has used propaganda, sabotage, assassination, bribery, proxy fronts, and false-flag operations to supplement its considerable conventional force posture in eastern Ukraine, where several thousand Russian military intelligence advisors, unit commanders, and flag officers exercise command and control over a separatist force consisting of roughly 30,000–40,000 troops.

Moscow has been doing its homework. Recognizing that Russia's conventional military capabilities lag behind those of NATO, Russian Chief of the General Staff Valeriy Gerasimov called in 2013 for investing in asymmetric capabilities to enable Russia to fight and win against conventionally superior Western militaries. Gerasimov's call for more emphasis on unconventional warfare also coincided with a subtle but important shift in Russian foreign policy. After Mr. Putin's return to the Kremlin in 2012, Moscow dispensed with its post-Cold War foreign policy of cooperating with the West where possible and competing where necessary. Instead, the Kremlin now actively seeks to corrode the institutions of Western democracy, undermine the transatlantic alliance, and delegitimize the liberal international order through a continuous and sustained competition short of conflict that takes place across all domains.

However, even with Russia's well-honed unconventional warfare capabilities, the United States and its NATO Allies can prevail in this competition if we recognize the Kremlin's goals for what they are, develop smart strategies to counter them, properly align our institutional structures, and invest in the right capabilities.

I will briefly discuss six areas where Russia has invested in significant unconventional or "new generation warfare" capabilities, and suggest some responses the United States should consider. All of the capabilities I will highlight were used during Russia's invasion of Ukraine in 2014 and remain on display as Russia continues to wage its unconventional war against the government in Kyiv.

INFORMATION WARFARE

First, Russia has demonstrated a mastery of the tools of information warfare. Russia's intelligence services understood through their "operational preparation of the environment" (OPE) how to tailor messages that would resonate with the population of eastern Ukraine. Such efforts began long before the Maidan protests as networks of influence were established across virtually all of Ukraine's government and military institutions, allowing for rapid activation once the conflict began. Immediately after President Yanukovych's ouster, Russian media outlets and government officials began to disseminate a narrative that Yanukovych had been forced out of power by Ukrainian fascists supported by the West. This propaganda was so insidious that even an 86-year-old Ukrainian-American living in the United States whose sole source of news is Russian TV could believe that a fascist government had come to power in Kyiv.

It is not just the message that matters, but also Russia's virtual monopoly of the medium. To guarantee its control of information, one of the first operations Russian special services carried out inside Ukraine in the spring of 2014 was to seize key television transmission towers. This monopoly on broadcast television lasted until only recently. In December 2016, Ukraine inaugurated a new television tower near Slovyansk to broadcast its own public programming into occupied eastern Ukraine, while Ukrainian public radio only began broadcasting into the Donbas in January 2017.

To counteract Russian propaganda, the United States needs to take a more pro-active approach.

United States European Command led the way during the Ukraine crisis by revealing de-classified images of Russian tanks and equipment, and NGOs [Non-Government Organizations] like Bellingcat followed suit with further proof of Russia's involvement, including evidence of Russia's role in the shoot-down of MH–17. However, more is needed beyond simply publicizing evidence of Russian aggression. The United States should consider making greater use of regulatory tools to label Russian propaganda for what it is, for example by mandating a screen banner warning viewers of RT [Russia Today] or Sputnik that they are watching Russian government programming. An independent commission should also be established to identify and take action against Russian misinformation. In parallel, the 2016 Countering Disinformation and Propaganda Act should be used to spur the development of a robust whole-of-government toolbox for exposing and countering Russian propaganda, ideally drawing on expertise outside of government.

Counter-disinformation strategies will also be more effective when coordinated across the NATO Alliance, particularly since Russian disinformation has found fertile ground in many European societies. Expanding the funding and mandate of the NATO Center of Excellence on Strategic Communications in Latvia would help share best practices on counter-messaging. The Center should also explore how to use big data analytics and other social media tools to counteract Russia's well-financed army of internet bots and trolls. For example, technological solutions should be explored, including "spam filters" for content generated by programmed bots.

Finally, the United States should not limit itself to refuting lies in the Western media space but should take a more active role in exposing lies and corruption within Russia. Those who claim Russian citizens are inured to revelations of high-level corruption or Russian military involvement in the war on Ukraine do not understand what the Kremlin knows well. Russian opposition politician Boris Nemtsov was murdered only a few hundred yards from the Kremlin in part because he had revealed information about the Russian military's direct involvement in the war in Ukraine. Exiled Duma lawmaker Denis Voronenkov was murdered last week in Kyiv because he was ready to speak about Russia's ties to Yanukovych and the war in Ukraine. The Russian NGO Soldiers' Mothers was declared an "undesirable foreign agent" by the Russian government after its members exposed the cover-up of Russian service-members' deaths in Ukraine. Clearly, the Kremlin does not want this information to be disseminated within Russia and is willing to go to extreme lengths to silence these voices. Protests across Russia just within the last few days also provide ample proof that Russian citizens do not accept corruption as a way of life.

To speak directly to Russian citizens and Russian speakers, the United States should devote more resources to projects like *Current Time,* the Broadcasting Board of Governors' new 24/7 Russian-language digital network, which provides information to Russians and Russian-speaking audiences on Russia's periphery. The United States should also consider supporting efforts like Estonia's Russian-language public television station, which has filled an important vacuum in the Baltic region's information space.

CYBER OPERATIONS

A second unconventional tool Russia is using to great effect in Ukraine is cyber-attacks, which range from "hacking" Ukrainian networks to steal information for intelligence or propaganda purposes to crippling denial of service attacks on critical infrastructure. At the start of the conflict, the deployment of Russian special forces to Crimea was accompanied by cyber-attacks on cellular and internet connections to disrupt the government's ability communicate with its citizens. Similar operations were launched in Georgia during Russia's invasion in August 2008. Cyber operations were also augmented by the use of electronic warfare equipment to block cellular and radio signals used by the Ukrainian Armed Forces as well as civilians.

Cyber-attacks against Ukraine have escalated since the conflict began. In December 2015, evidence shows Russia hacked into the Supervisory Control and Data Acquisition (SCADA) networks of two Ukrainian energy companies, shutting off electricity and heat for a brief period before Ukraine was able to restore power. The attacks on the SCADA systems were accompanied by distributed denial of service (DDOS) attacks on telephone-operated customer call centers so complaints of a power outage would not get through to company operators. However, even when Russia was identified as the perpetrator of this attack, it was not deterred. In December 2016, Ukraine's power grid suffered another cyber-attack, and Russian cyber actors separately targeted Ukraine's payments system for government salaries and pensions. These attacks should serve as a wake-up call for the West, particularly since many Western power companies lack the backup manual functionality that helped Ukraine avert what could have otherwise been a crippling power shutoff. The potential for disruptive cyber action is enormous and deterrence is complicated by the difficulty of attribution. While recent discussions of Russia's cyber-attacks in the United States have focused on hacking and disclosure of information, we must not overlook the fact that Russia's cyber weapons have a potential lethality and scope that is matched only by strategic nuclear weapons.

The Defense Department must therefore invest more in United States Cyber Command's capabilities, and the United States should also continue to help build our Allies' and partners' cyber-defenses, which in many cases are more vulnerable than our own. Election-day attacks in Montenegro in October 2016 not only spread disinformation about the election on social media platforms such as Viber and WhatsApp, but also targeted the Ministry of Defense's network. At a December meeting of the United States-Adriatic Charter, defense ministers from across the Balkans noted their cyber defenses needed to be urgently upgraded in the face of increased Russian cyber activity.

United States-based efforts should also include stronger regulatory oversight to ensure standards are met for hardening critical infrastructure against cyber intrusions and attacks since much of this effort is currently left at the discretion of the private corporations that manage this infrastructure. Admiral Stavridis' suggestion to establish a National Cyber Academy is also worth considering, and the Defense Department's public-private partnerships with the information technology sector, like the Defense Innovation Unit Experimental (DIUx) launched by former Secretary of Defense Carter, should be expanded.

Finally, in cases where NATO or the United States are able to attribute a specific attack, the response must be timely and proportionate to deter future attacks. In the case of the cyber-attack against the United States during the presidential election, the declaration of Russian intelligence officials as *persona non grata* (PNG) is unfortunately a largely symbolic action with few lasting consequences given that these positions will soon be backfilled with other operatives. As long as Russian cyber actors encounter weak resistance, the Kremlin will continue to leverage its cyber capabilities against the West.

CLANDESTINE AND COVERT OPERATIONS

Third, Russia's intervention in Ukraine demonstrates a mastery of the art of clandestine and covert operations. During its armed takeover of government buildings and military installations in Crimea in 2014, Russia deliberately chose to deploy what are now known as "little green men," or special forces in uniforms without insignias. The deployment of these semi-overt, semi-covert forces allowed Russia to maintain the fiction on the international stage that the conflict involved only local actors. At the same time, it made perfectly clear to those on the ground that the troops were in fact highly capable Russian special forces. Through this "asymmetric ambiguity" Russia was able to stave off the international community's immediate condemnation while simultaneously deterring Ukraine's interim government from fighting back. In essence, the Russian General Staff set the same trap it used in Georgia in 2008 when it covertly deploy special forces to create unrest: if the host government fights back and there are casualties, then the Kremlin is handed a pretext for launching a war to protect Russian compatriots; if the host government chooses not to fight, Russian forces have a free hand. In either case, Russia wins.

In addition to its semi-overt "little green men," Russia also deployed true covert operators to the Donbas. These "little gray men" organized and sometimes even led demonstrations and seizures of government buildings and police stations across eastern Ukraine in the spring of 2014. In April 2014, for example, Russian covert actors organized the seizure of the Kharkiv Opera House, which they mistakenly believed was City Hall, using paid protestors who had been bussed in from outside the city. A deadlier and more tragic incident occurred in May 2014 when pro-Kremlin protestors barricaded themselves inside a building in the port city of Odessa, which was then set on fire.

Importantly, Russia's covert agents were far less successful in stoking separatist sentiments in other parts of southern and eastern Ukraine than they were in Crimea. Thanks to the social resilience of the local population and more effective local law enforcement operations, Russian-directed efforts to foment anti-government insurgencies failed in major cities like Kharkiv, Odessa, Dnipro, and Mariupol. Russia's recent attempted coup d'état in Montenegro is also illustrative of how effective collaboration between intelligence and law enforcement agencies can thwart such covert operations. In the Montenegrin case, Russian military intelligence officers recruited mercenaries among far-right nationalist groups in Serbia and local criminal elements and hatched a plan for them to fire on anti-government protestors on election day while wearing stolen Montenegrin police uniforms. Fortunately, a tip-off and good intelligence work prevented the plot from moving forward as planned.

More broadly, defeating or neutralizing influence operations requires strengthening societal resilience through government programs that build stronger ties to disaffected ethnic groups or communities that are less well integrated into a country's social fabric. This requires a "wholeof-government" approach that coordinates among ministries of defense, internal affairs, and intelligence bodies, as well as health, social, and economic agencies. Finally, awareness of the threat is critical. In the Ukrainian case, Russia's operation in Crimea was successful in part (though there were other reasons) because it occurred first. Once Ukrainian citizens became aware that Russian forces were intervening militarily in their country, subsequent operations proved much more difficult even in areas where there were historically high levels of distrust in the central government. Within NATO it is vital for the Alliance to develop Indicators and Warnings (I&W) that rely not only on military factors, but also on social trends and dynamics.

PROXY FORCES

Fourth, Russia relies on a range of proxy groups to carry out subversive actions and fight as irregular forces. In Ukraine, these groups include local organized criminal groups, Yanukovychregime thugs known as *tytushki,* former Berkut riot police, Cossacks and Chechen fighters who came from Russia, members of the infamous Russian "Night Wolves" motorcycle gang, and a smattering of Russian and East European neo-Nazi volunteers. This medley of proxy groups proved to be little match initially for Ukraine's conventional military in the summer of 2014, during which Ukrainian forces succeeded in retaking significant territory. However, when it appeared that Ukraine might actually defeat the separatist forces, Russia intervened with a large number of conventional brigade combat teams that were ready and waiting in staging areas near the Ukrainian border.

Even after the tragic defeat of Ukrainian forces in Ilovaysk in August 2014, the Russian military encountered considerable difficulties with command and control of its proxies. Rampant criminality also prevailed as the various proxy groups organized themselves into mini-fiefdoms. This led the Kremlin to send high-level emissaries to reign in the various warlords, and when that failed special forces even resorted to assassination and forced extraction from the battlefield. The leader of the Cossack Great Don Army, Nikolai Kozitsyn, was for example forced out of the Donbas by Russian services. Another prominent Russian commander, Igor Strelkov (aka Igor Girkin), was also removed. To instill greater professionalism among its proxy forces, therefore, Moscow has increasingly turned in both Ukraine and Syria to private military companies.

I would contend that Moscow's greatest success with proxy groups has not been on the battlefield but on the diplomatic stage. Using the Geneva International Discussions on Georgia as a model, the Kremlin has insisted that no negotiations take place without the involvement of proxy leaders. One of the biggest mistakes made by the Western leaders of the "Normandy Group" (France, Germany, Ukraine, Russia) was to agree to Russia's demands and elevate the role of Russian proxies in the February 2015 Minsk Protocol. By establishing a parallel negotiation process involving proxies, Russia has largely been able to evade blame for its failure to implement even the most basic elements of the Minsk agreement: ceasefire, withdrawal of heavy weapons, and unlimited access for OSCE [Organization for Security and Co-operation in Europe] monitors to the territory of the Donbas. The result is a kabuki negotiation led by the OSCE in which the proxies stonewall any meaningful progress on implementing the agreement. So long as this dynamic is maintained and Moscow is able to hide behind the claim that local leaders are to blame for the impasse, the conflict will almost certainly continue unabated. Conversely, the sooner the international community cuts through the fiction that local actors call all the shots and applies pressure on Moscow, the closer we will be to a real negotiation aimed at resolving the conflict.

SABOTAGE AND TERRORISM

Sabotage and acts of terrorism have also been used in the Ukraine conflict. On the same day that former Duma member Denis Voronenkov was assassinated in Kyiv, an act of sabotage destroyed a large munition depot in Balaklia, forcing the evacuation of 20,000 civilians form nearby areas. Earlier in the conflict, Ukraine's security service, the SBU, accused Russia of having orchestrated a bombing attack on a rally in Kharkiv in February 2015 that killed a policeman and a civilian as well as bombing attacks on railroads, a courtroom, a pub frequented by pro-Maidan supporters, and the offices of a pro-Maidan NGO. Given the long border between Russia and Ukraine and extensive societal and family ties between the two countries, preventing acts of terrorism and sabotage remains difficult and relies heavily on good intelligence and societal resilience.

POLITICAL AND ECONOMIC SUBVERSION

Finally, political and economic subversion have increasingly become Russia's favored method of seeking to exert control over the government in Kyiv. Indeed, Russia has increased its political influence operations not just in Ukraine but throughout Europe and the United States, seeing them as a cheaper and more effective way to achieve its aims in the gray zone. Unconventional military operations carry a significant degree of risk, while political influence operations are easier to carry out and are camouflaged behind an often convoluted faade of corrupt business and political ties.

As part of this subversive campaign, Russia's intelligence services and Kremlin-linked oligarchs have targeted Western political parties, businessmen, politicians, media organizations, and NGOs. The goal is not always to influence a near-term political outcome, but sometimes simply to burrow into a country's political and economic fabric. In this way, corrupt ties and *kompromat* (material for blackmail) can be built up in reserve and deployed at the opportune moment. The primary tool used in these influence operations is Russia's vast network of corrupt patron-client relations, which extend not only to the former Soviet space but also to Europe and the United States. Russian businessmen who have professional ties in a particular country can be "encouraged" to donate money to select NGOs, offshore companies can be used to funnel money to political parties, and Russian cultural organizations such as state-run *Rossotrudnichestvo* can be used to forge ties with pro-Kremlin diaspora groups. Money laundering schemes using shell companies or "one-day firms" help to channel the flow of licit and illicit money from these various actors to favored politicians, NGOs, and media organizations.

To counteract this rising tide of Russian political subversion, Western states need to build more transparent institutions, particularly with regards to political party financing, and empower anti-corruption organizations, financial investigation units, and law enforcement bodies to coordinate with intelligence organizations to root out entrenched and corrosive Russian patronage networks. The United States should seriously consider establishing a standing interagency operational body dedicated solely to interdicting illicit Russian influence operations. Current interagency efforts to track Russian malign influence are not sufficient because of the firewall between policy agencies like the State Department and National Security Council on the one hand, and law enforcement bodies on the other.

On the policy side, the United States must also make better use of the tools already at its disposal. Financial sanctions against Russia remain vastly under-utilized given the scope of financial leverage the United States has over Russia. To date, the United States has only applied full blocking sanctions on one Russian bank, and that bank is not even among the 20 largest Russian financial institutions. Furthermore, personal sanctions against corrupt individuals such as those mandated by the Magnitsky Act have barely been utilized at all, with less than 30 individuals designated since 2012.

Finally, in the United States it is vital that an independent Special Prosecutor be empowered to investigate allegations of ties between the Russian Government and United States political actors. Of all the lessons from Russia's influence operations in Ukraine and elsewhere in Europe, this one impinges most directly on our national security. It is frankly impossible to understand how one could point to vulnerabilities among our Allies and partners while neglecting to thoroughly and impartially investigate Russia's influence operation right here in the United States.

CONCLUSION

The effort to counter Russia's operations in the gray zone should start in Ukraine, where Moscow continues to fight an unconventional war against Kyiv. To check Russian influence in Ukraine, the United States must dedicate more resources to bolster military training programs for Ukraine's conventional and special operations forces. It should provide Ukraine with defensive weapons such as anti-tank missiles and equipment such as counter-battery radars with advanced fire control systems and more effective Intelligence, Surveillance, and Reconnaissance (ISR) platforms. On the diplomatic front, the United States cannot afford to remain a spectator as the Normandy Group engages in endless negotiations. The United States must get involved in these negotiations and help the parties develop a concrete roadmap of actions to implement the two Minsk agreements of September 2014 and February 2015. Crucially, this roadmap must specify specific dates by which actions must be completed and consequences for failing to meet required deadlines. To sharpen United States leverage, the United States should consider unilaterally tightening current debt and equity restrictions on Russian financial institutions, and if necessary incrementally apply blocking sanctions to signal resolve. Positive incentives should also be offered for compliance with the Minsk roadmap. Lastly, the United States needs to continue to support Ukraine's reforms, in part by applying strict conditionality to United States assistance and insisting on Ukrainian follow-through, but also by encouraging our European partners to play a more active role in supporting reform.

As we consider more robust measures to push back on Russian influence operations in Ukraine and elsewhere in Europe, we cannot blind ourselves to the painful fact that these operations have been targeted at the United States as well. I have argued before that if Russian aggression in places like Georgia and Ukraine is not checked, Russian malign influence will continue to spread to our allies in Europe as well as here in the United States. Now it is a fact that Russia has sought to corrode one of the most sacred institutions in this country: our democratic process. We must be prepared to respond with the sense of seriousness and urgency that is required.

Senator ERNST. Thank you, Dr. Carpenter.
Lieutenant General Cleveland.

STATEMENT OF LIEUTENANT GENERAL CHARLES T. CLEVELAND, USA (RET.), SENIOR FELLOW, MADISON POLICY FORUM, AND FORMER COMMANDING GENERAL, UNITED STATES ARMY SPECIAL OPERATIONS COMMAND

General CLEVELAND. Thank you. Chairman Ernst, Ranking Member Heinrich, members of the subcommittee, thank you for the opportunity to share some thoughts, some old-guy thoughts as I would say, on unconventional warfare, population-centric warfare, and the challenges the United States faces encountering nontraditional or nonconventional strategies.

Russia's success in Crimea and its actions in eastern Ukraine have caused the world rightly to take note. Through the creative use of violence and threats, Russia redrew, as was mentioned earlier, the international boundaries for the first time in decades. Its success to date is destabilizing an international system that had put in check the territorial ambitions of its members. Disturbing is the fact that they were so successful without paying much of a price, at least politically, as Putin remains popular with his people. The United States military's response has been appropriate and if

not predictable. Increased exercises engaged in joint planning learn from Ukraine and try to find and apply countermeasures in the Baltics. In the last few years, though, I would submit not only from that experience but from my experiences around the world, we have learned a few things. We have learned that the limits of our understanding of foreign cultures matter. We have learned how important that understanding is to developing viable security policies and responses. We have learned the limits of our funding authorities and the inadequacies of some of our existing civilian and military organizations and their understanding of indigenous-centric warfighting. We have learned the inadequacy of our current ability to use psychological and information operations, which has been mentioned earlier. We have learned the hard lesson of the inelastic element of time in these population-centric wars.

But these limitations obviously are not just with Russia and its nefariousness. It is in fact with actors that are practicing this form of warfare around the world. I would submit that our lack of understanding of this form of warfare has helped lead to poor results in Iraq and Afghanistan as well, and have limited our thinking and options in Syria, Yemen, and pretty much everywhere population-centric wars are being fought.

I offer the following eight points: First, recognize that these population-centric wars are different from traditional war. Two dangerous myths are that such wars are only a lesser case of traditional war or, to the contrary, these are graduate levels of the same war. Neither is correct and both lead to bad assumptions that we can be successful by just doing better with what we have got or go bigger with what we have got or invest more money more wisely.

We have a laundry list of alphabet soup ad hoc structures created over the past 16 years. It was the battlefield's way of telling us that what we brought to those fights was not enough. New models, concepts, and resulting doctrine organizations and leaders and soldiers are needed in my view, particularly above the tactical level.

Secondly, whatever America's new strategy works out to be, I sincerely hope, as one who lived my life under the special forces motto of de oppresso liber, that it does not relegate hundreds of millions of people around the world to tyranny. The inevitable instability that would result would force our involvement anyway, given as interconnected as the world is today. So it is better that we proactively gain an understanding, shape and act in concert with like-minded friends, partners, and allies, providing leadership when necessary and inspirational always.

Consensus on a national strategy beyond simply an open-ended fascination with CT [counter-terrorism] is critical for providing direction and clarity. Containment was a powerful centering concepts that helped drive security-sector efforts. It was perhaps practiced differently between the political parties, but by and large it remained an organizing principle throughout the Cold War. Whatever comes next, my recommendation, given the instability in the system and the provocations by regional actors and non-state groups, that it be underpinned by an unmatched soft indigenous-centric and direct-action warfighting capability, superior and elite high-end conventional forces, and a robust diplomatic core.

Third, organize around the reality of modern political warfare or, as my lawyer preferred to call it, unconventional diplomacy. Russia, China, Iran are each employing these forms of political warfare and calls for the United States to relearn lessons from the Cold War on its own approach to political warfare are worth serious consideration. For example, our acknowledged problems conducting effective information campaigns might improve with a 21st century variation of the United States Information Agency.

Some other ideas are, one, ensure that the NFC has UW [unconventional warfare] expertise or unconventional warfare expertise; two, create a Deputy Assistant Secretary of Defense for Special Warfare, that being unconventional warfare to foreign internal defense or population-centric warfighting; at the State Department, create a bureau for political warfare led by an official of ambassadorial rank similar to what they have done with counterterrorism; and four, create the creation of a joint special warfare command within SOCOM [Special Operations Command] that would hopefully match the success of its direct-action counterpart. It would be an interagency command with perhaps a deputy from another agency, another government agency or state and other interagency officers serving as fully empowered members on a tailored headquarter staff.

The TSOCs or the Theater Special Operations Commands, currently COCOM [combatant command] to SOCOM, could be subordinated to such a headquarters, freeing the SOCOM staff to focus on their policy procurement, joint soft doctrine development, and unit-readiness missions. This structure would give more weight to SOCOM's unconventional warfare of foreign internal defense, civil affairs, and psychological operations or military information support operations by providing a single headquarters that would, by necessity, be the advocate for U.S. support to indigenous warfighting, unconventional warfare, and foreign internal defense.

SOCOM has concentrated money and effort rightly towards building an exquisite direct action capability, but other of its legislative missions have suffered, particularly, in my view, information operations.

Fourth, the U.S. has been seeking the holy grail of whole-of-government warfighting for well over 50 years. Presidents have issued several decision directives to get at this, but it remains elusive. There must be an outside forcing function to do better in my mind. Putin's success directly reflects the Russian hold on all levels of government and the elements of power outside of government and their adept use, resulting in a sophisticated, complex, hybrid war or unconventional warfare campaign. Certainly that is easier for an authoritarian government. But the stovepiped authorization and appropriation of funds creates internal pressures that work against developing cross-department solutions. Add to that the different cultures of the security sector departments and agencies, and it is rare to see any real moves towards creating a truly interagency solution.

It is fair to ask the question who funds whole-of-government or whole-of-nation solutions to a problem? We do not. Instead, we fund in pieces and parts. Department and agency projects entrust they come together somewhere to get the job done. Congress may want to look at funding incentives to promote collective planning.

Fifth, recognize that our critical weaknesses and gaps in defense are above the tactical level. Our standing campaign-level headquarters, primarily the U.S. Army Corps and U.S. Marine Corps MEFs [Marine Expeditionary Forces] are rightly organized around conventional warfighting. The one operational-level SOF headquarters is primarily organized around the counterterrorism and direct action mission, as it needs to be.

A dedicated operational-level headquarters around the execution of indigenous-centric campaign such as Iraq and Syria today is merited. A hybrid soft conventional interagency U.S. Army base core that is designed for complex contingency merits consideration. These kinds of operations are no longer the aberration but in fact are the norm. We should organize accordingly.

Six, develop the 12XX funding authority like 1208 for CT, for soft formations now need access to funds to develop indigenous UW capabilities obviously approved by the country team, obviously approved by the geographic combatant commander in an approved campaign on the part of the United States or the foreign internal defense appropriate capabilities to counter a hostile country's unconventional warfare threats that are not CT-related.

Seven, the most prevalent forms of competition and conflict around the world today are resistance, rebellion, and insurgency. They manifest themselves oftentimes in the use of the tactic of terror and, if successful, they culminate in civil war. Yet despite its prevalence, DOD has no professional military education dedicated to these forms of warfare, the service's own professional military education responsibility for their soldiers, sailors, airmen, and marines. The result is that a deep understanding of these conflicts, these most prevalent forms of war, within the ranks depends primarily on the individual initiative of the leader. There are some electives at the various command and staff in war colleges but the net result is that military leaders get very little formal education on this form of war.

More concerning to me is the fact that our Special Forces, Civil Affairs, and SIOP officers, and those who eventually become the leaders who learn the basics of population-centric warfighting in their qualifications course, but from that point on are in a professional military education program focused on essentially conventional warfighting.

Those who attended Army schools appreciated the—those of us who attended the Army schools appreciated the year at Command and General Staff College and the Army War College, both institutions of which I am a graduate, and I appreciated the year with our conventional counterparts and some of the lessons certainly that are universally important to warfighting. But it did not make me much better really at the form of warfighting that I was to practice on behalf of the Nation. SOCOM or the Army—in my view SOCOM should create a career-long professional development path for those who are charged with being expert at indigenous warfighting.

Point number eight and my last point is we are the good guys. You know, our asymmetry again in my view is who we are and from where the United States Government and this great nation derives its strength. While Russia, China, and Iran must control their people, the strength of our country is our people and their belief in our form of government, the inalienable rights granted by our Creator, the guarantees of life, liberty, and the pursuit of happiness. I think that provides us and those that are privileged enough to have this as a form of government around the world the resilience that Dr. Carpenter was talking about in our social structure.

A deep understanding and commitment to the development and maintenance of world-class unconventional warfare capability can be a powerful tool in countering the use of surrogates in hybrid warfare by revisionist and revolutionary movements. It has the potential to impose costs on them. It holds them at risk. In addition to providing an offensive capability from which we can learn and stay abreast of the art and science of warfighting, it is in fact I think necessary as we see the evidence of an emerging domain— a new emerging domain of war, the human domain.

I am not optimistic, however, that DOD can address its deficiencies. It will need Congress' help. We should be asking on behalf of the American taxpayer if we knew in early 2002 what we know now, what would we do differently? What has SOCOM, the Army, and the Marine Corps as land components learned these last 16 years, and what does that portend for the future?

Multidomain battle might be the beginnings of a replacement for air-land battle but only if we acknowledge in my view that the human domain, this place where insurgencies, resistance, and rebellion happen, takes its place along the traditional four domains, land, sea, air, and space, and the newly acknowledged cyber. It appears in fact in my view the Russians have learned this lesson and are getting better at it, as we continue to admire the problem.

Thank you, Madam Chairman.

Senator ERNST. Thank you to our witnesses.

We will start with our rounds of questions, and we will limit those to five minutes of questions and answers per Senator.

General Cleveland, if I could start with you, why were the Russians so successful in achieving their objectives of illegally annexing Crimea and destabilizing eastern Ukraine, and why do you think United States special operations forces are prepared today to counter situations like that in the future?

General CLEVELAND. Ma'am, I am not sure—I mean, the Russians had a tremendous home-field advantage in Crimea, and we would have had to recognize and understand alongside the Ukrainian Government early, early on what was happening. I am not sure that we had our antenna out to be sensitive to that and then be able to react early enough to counter what was going on using many of the things that were spoken about earlier, being transparent, you know, shaming, bringing that out, providing perhaps some information warfare antidote to just the blitzkrieg, as was described on the information front.

I think that special operations forces today, as you have noted in your opener, we have been focused primarily on the CT mission. However, there is an element within SOCOM in the special operations community which has been applying its trade in indigenous warfighting that maybe earlier on, had we had the political will to commit to supporting the Ukrainian Government in its early, early stages, we could have at least been a tripwire. We could have perhaps provided some capability. We would have shown perhaps resolve that we would not let this type of nefariousness stand.

But that is a policy decision. That is what you all get paid the big bucks for. So, again—but I think that the tools were there. Whether they were considered in the deliberations and whether those that were in a position to advise were literate enough to provide what those options might look like, that I do not know. I was obviously focused still at Fort Bragg.

Senator ERNST. Absolutely. Thank you very much, General. I appreciate it.

Dr. Carpenter, to counter Russian information operations, you say that the United States should take a more proactive approach, including identifying and taking action against Russian misinformation or debunking those false stories, and I agree with you on that point. Can you explain to us what role the messaging in Russian films and TV shows plays into this information campaign, and then also what about social media and how that applies to the situation?

Dr. CARPENTER. Well, Russia has made great use of the virtual monopoly that it has on broadcast television inside Russia but then also in occupied parts of Ukraine to be able to get its message out. It relies on very slick programming that appeals to the folks that tune into TV. It is shows, it is other—it is comedy, it is movies, but then it is also interspersed with propaganda. It is very difficult to combat when most people in these areas get their sources of information from TV.

I think the way to go about combating that is to try to go and use the various platforms that we have available to get the message out in this information space. So I would actually separate this into two things. There are things that we need to do here in the United States so we have RT, we have Sputnik, which are Russia propaganda programs here in the United States. Frankly, I would advocate using more regulatory tools to, for example, put a banner at the bottom of the screen saying this programming is financed by the Russian Government or is Russian Government programming so the people are aware. We still protect the First Amendment rights to watch what they want to watch, but they are aware just like we do with cigarette packages to warn them what it is that is inside the package.

In Russia and inside occupied Ukraine, it is a little bit more difficult. The BBG [Broadcasting Board of Governors] has developed some digital tools so that is programming that is now available on a 24/7 basis that can get inside to Russia, but it is available on the internet. Most people still tune into broadcast TV to get their news and to get sources of information.

But we need to push more. We need to get out a message not just—we cannot just play whack-a-mole and continuously try to debunk every single fake news story that Russia puts out there. That puts us on the defensive. We need to start to put out information about what is going on in Russia in terms of corruption. You see the protests that just took place on Sunday across almost 100 cities within Russia, and so I think getting the message out will resonate in Russian society.

It is just simply a matter of letting people know what is actually happening with their government. I think a lot of Russians to this day believe the government in Kyiv is run by fascists. They believe all kinds of fake news stories that have been peddled simply because they do not have an alternative source of information. So we need to get better at that.

The Baltic States have also been good at putting out some broadcast programming that aims at Russian-speaking audiences. It is limited to the Baltic region, but we should explore supporting them and trying to get that broadcasting out to more Russian speakers.

Senator ERNST. Very good. Thank you.

Ranking Member Heinrich?

Senator HEINRICH. Dr. Carpenter, what would be the technological limitations or other limitations to allow us to reach people on broadcast television as opposed to the internet platform from some of those neighboring states?

Dr. CARPENTER. So I think——

Senator HEINRICH. What kind of reach could we foreseeably actually have?

Dr. CARPENTER. So I think it is very difficult to be able to broadcast into Russia itself because they control the means of both blocking foreign broadcasting and, as I said, they have a virtual monopoly on this. But that does not mean that we should not try, especially in regions like the Baltic. I was told by those who lived through the Soviet experience in the Baltics that those who lived near the Polish border would tune in to Polish TV, they would listen to—even though Polish TV was also part of the Warsaw Pact, it was also propagandistic. But it was more open than Soviet television, and so they would listen, and then they would transmit those messages to friends and acquaintances and spread it through their social networks.

I think if you have broadcast programs in the Baltic, in Ukraine, in Moldova, in Georgia, in places on Russia's periphery, it will seep into Russia. It may not be as effective as if you had broadcast television in Moscow and St. Petersburg, but it will go a long way. I think the Russian people actually crave more information, and when they are exposed to it, they will benefit.

Senator HEINRICH. On a sort of related question, and this is really for any of you, given Russian employment of disinformation and digital trolls and bots in Western elections, including our own last year, and the fact that the issue that you, Dr. Oliker, brought up of people preferring their own information sources and discounting all others is certainly not limited to Europe. We see that very much the case in the United States today, people self-selecting information sources and almost living in parallel universes.

What lessons can we learn actually from countries like Estonia and others that have been on the frontlines of this dual world for longer than we have and have developed a sensitivity to the manipulations of the Russian Government? How can we take some of the lessons that they have had and utilize them in our own self-awareness of what is going on here and now? This is for any of you really.

Dr. OLIKER. Thank you. I would actually say, you know, I was watching the protests in Russia on Sunday. One of the things that is most striking about them was the number of youth that were out there. The protests we saw in Russia in 2011 and 2012 were mostly middle-aged and older folks. This was a lot of young people. This is very preliminary, but my sense is they do not get their information from television. They get their information from the internet, from each other. The other thing we saw before the protest was some reports of conversations of faculty and students in Russian schools, which also evidenced a certain amount of critical thinking.

So I think there are actually lessons we can take from Russia here that—and I do not—you know, I do not know that governments can do this well but I think the private sector may be able to, which is about figuring out how to target youth, recognizing that youth are bright and are discerning and are, you know, perhaps intrinsically distrustful of what older people tell them and using that— not so much using it as a propaganda tool of the United States Government but creating in the marketplace of ideas a real market for truth.

I think that is something—and we in the United States and our partners and allies in Europe can help support our private sector in doing that. But I very strongly do not think this is a government task.

Senator HEINRICH. Do either of the rest of you have an opinion about what lessons we might learn from some of our allies like Estonia?

Dr. CARPENTER. So I would just say that we do need to get much more savvy about using social media to reach out to Russian youth. I do not think it necessarily has to be a government-funded website or a government-run social media platform, but providing the content to others to be able to disseminate I think is important.

To give you an anecdote, about a year and a half ago there was a woman in the Russian city of Yekaterinburg who was putting— on her personal blog she was just simply putting stories from Reuters and AP [Associated Press] on what was happening in Ukraine, and she was charged with treason and put in jail. So this demonstrates to me that the Russian Government is extremely sensitive to having this information even on a digital platform, even on a blog, and reacts accordingly.

I think if we can get the information out there and, yes, it tends to be clunky when it is run by government public institutions, but there are ways we can partner with more commercial, private, sleeker outfits that are able to get the message out, and I think it will have a great effect if we do that.

Senator HEINRICH. Thank you.

Senator ERNST. Senator Peters.

Senator PETERS. Thank you, Madam Chair.

I would like to expand some of the conversation and, Dr. Oliker, you brought this up is that, as troublesome as the Russian activities are, and they are very troublesome, it also I think indicates that we have some greater vulnerabilities across the globe in terms of some of the weakness in institutions that are essential. In fact, I think in your written testimony you talk about the only way we really protect ourselves and others against this is to have strong institutions.

I was struck by the Munich Security Conference, which I had an opportunity to attend, and the theme of that was post-truth, post-order, and post-West, which are all pretty scary concepts to think about, moving away from order and away from truth. If you do not have truth, how do you survive as a democratic society?

In your testimony you talk about how the Russians do exploit those sorts of weaknesses with institutions. Could you explain a little bit or elaborate on where you think the greatest vulnerabilities are with our institutions and how do we strengthen them?

Dr. OLIKER. I think right now the greatest vulnerability in our institutions is our own move away from truth. The stooping to the same level, the shift to an effort to influence rather than an effort to inform, and I think also affected very heavily by the way that the internet-based news cycle creates a demand for information now before it has been processed and understood. I do not have a great solution for that one.

I do think that, over time, accountability, transparency, and to some extent regulation can make a real difference, but I do think our greatest vulnerability is that if everybody plays this game of muddying the waters, the people who are best at muddying the waters are going to win, and that is not going to be us.

I also think that our institutions have additional weaknesses which are that they were created for a different situation. I think our institutions do need reforms and they do need strengthening and they do need to be adapted for the situations we find ourselves in. Here I am talking about international institutions. I am talking about NATO. I think these things have served us tremendously well for a very long time. We are finding that people are not satisfied with the extent to which they serve them now, and I think it is important to look at how to adapt them.

I also think that in Europe we know that Russia does not feel it is served well by the institutions that have sprung up since the end of the Cold War, and Russia has not been happy about this for 25 years. I am not saying we appease the Russians. I do say that, as long as they feel insecure, we are going to continue to have a problem.

Senator PETERS. Well, if you look at the playbook of how someone who wants to take advantage of these vulnerabilities, we have seen the playbook before. You go after the press. You try to delegitimize the press and say it is all fake news. It is just not real and attack it. You keep people of certain press organizations out of press conferences, let us say, because you attack them. You attack the judiciary. You say there are so-called judges or folks of their certain ethnic background, and then you can operate perhaps when an institution that has to step up and actually be a counterbalancing institution like the

United States Congress that refuses to really bring light and bring transparency when we know there have been activities that have undermined our basic democracy.

Is that why, Dr. Carpenter, you believe that we have to have a special prosecutor when we know we have direct attacks on our democracy? If we are asking other countries to improve their institutions, to bring more transparency, how do we make that argument when we are not willing to do it ourselves?

Dr. CARPENTER. Well, I think we absolutely have to do it ourselves, and in fact I would unpack that and say I think there are a couple of separate things that we need to do to get precisely at this corruption of our institutional base. One is I think we absolutely need an independent special prosecutor to look at alleged ties between the Russian Government in the Trump campaign. I mean that to me—we have advised other countries—one of the conditions for Montenegro to get into NATO was that they establish an independent special prosecutor, and then when Russia attacked Montenegro on election day with an attempted coup d'état and cyber attacks——

Senator PETERS. Right.

Dr. CARPENTER.—that special prosecutor was then brought in to investigate and has done a standup job in doing so. If we can advise Montenegro to do that, we need to be able to have the political will to do that here at home.

But I also think that in addition to investigating this particular instance of Russian interference in our electoral process, I think we need a 9/11-style commission as well to look at Russian influence operations in the United States writ large and what we can do about it. It will be independent. It will have time, not focus narrowly on the prosecution of this particular case, but look at a broader writ and examine what Russia is doing and how we can combat it.

Finally, as I have said in my testimony, I think we need to stand up an operational body that is composed of interagency players that is dedicated—so within government, separate from the 9/11-style commission—that will look at Russian influence operations and how to counter them.

Right now, we have a number of groups in the State Department, in the Pentagon. I participated in them. I can tell you they are largely talk shops that try to diagnose the problem. They do not necessarily propose solutions, and they are not resourced to be able to do anything about it. So we need to have this sort of operational group that can specifically go after instances where we know Russia is interfering in our process and then try and eradicate that.

Senator PETERS. Thank you.

Senator ERNST. Senator Fischer.

Senator FISCHER. Thank you, Madam Chair.

Dr. Carpenter and Dr. Oliker, I assume that you both believe that Russia is going to attempt another gray zone provocation? First of all, is that correct?

Dr. OLIKER. I think eventually almost certainly. I think, you know, again, it depends on how you define the gray zone. If we are looking at action across borders that involve some military, quasi-military activity, I am probably looking at Moldova and Belarus more than I am looking at the Baltics.

I do think that when the Russians do it, it is not a—oh, I do not think the Russians are sitting around thinking where can we create a provocation. I do think that they tend to respond to what they see as threats to them with actions and sometimes actions in different areas, what we call horizontal escalation where you are attacked on one front and you respond on another. I do think they are looking for point of weakness where they might do that.

I do not think that for them Crimea and east Ukraine started out intentionally as a provocation of the United States, the West, and the global order. They were thinking of themselves very genuinely as defending their interests. When they realized, though, that they could affect the system that way, I think they got excited.

Senator FISCHER. Before you answer, Dr. Carpenter, if I could just follow up. You said not the Baltics but Belarus and Moldova. Does that follow along with a comment you made then also that it may not be where they feel a direct threat but kind of a—I do not know if you would say it is a diversion, a softball over someplace else to divert attention or just an opportunity presents itself in another country instead of where they might really be focused?

Dr. OLIKER. So I think that the Russians are deterred in the Baltics pretty effectively. The Russians would not have been so neurologically afraid of the incredibly unlikely contingency of Ukraine joining NATO if they did not believe in NATO. So, first point. The Russians have pretty much accepted the Baltics are gone.

This said, I think if the Russians feel that NATO is sufficiently weakened that there is a question there. There are certainly people in Russia who might develop designs on the Baltics. Right now, they are concerned about the Baltics, they are concerned about a Western military buildup there, they are worried about Kaliningrad. But if you look at it from their perspective and the way they write and talk about it, it is about the Western threat to them.

I think they also are spread thin enough with their operations in Ukraine and Syria with that, and they recognize the possibility that Ukraine might evolve to require even more, that they are not that interested right now in doing too much elsewhere. I could be wrong on that, but on the one hand they claim that they have very high manning levels. On the other, they have instituted a six-month contract. They do not send conscripts into combat but they are letting people sign a contract to become official military for just six months, which I take to mean they are having a hard time staffing even the limited contingencies they are in, which makes it very difficult to stretch.

Senator FISCHER. Dr. Carpenter, your thoughts, please.

Dr. CARPENTER. I guess I take a little bit of issue with that. I would distinguish between whether you are looking to understand whether Russia would carry out an operation like that in Crimea involving little green men, special forces in uniforms without insignias or whether we are talking about something a little bit even more covert than that, which is little gray men, the sorts of intelligence operatives who directed the seizure of buildings in the Donbas in the spring of 2014.

I think if you are talking about the latter, I think it is ongoing throughout Europe. I think we see influence operations of various degrees happening as we speak obviously in Ukraine but also in Georgia, in Moldova. If you look back just a couple years ago, an Estonian senior law-enforcement official was abducted from Estonian territory—now, this is a NATO ally—and taken to Russia. That was in a sense a gray zone provocation. It was not little green men crossing the border, but it was intelligence agents crossing the border and abducting and kidnapping.

As I mentioned in my testimony, there was an assassination last week, exactly a week ago today, in central Kyiv of an exiled Duma member because he was revealing information about Russian Government ties to both Yanukovych and also the start of the war in Ukraine.

These operations are happening each and every day sub rosa. But do I also worry about the potential for something that is more military that involves special forces either in or out of uniform? I do. I think that there is—I think Belarus right now is also very vulnerable, although it is very closely aligned with Russia geopolitically.

I think Russia believes that Belarus has strayed a little bit outside of the orbit, and it has therefore planned and exercised in September of this year Zapad 2017 where it has requisitioned 83 times the number of railcars to go into Belarus than it did when it last did this exercise in 2013. Something there does not add up in terms of just purely this being a traditional exercise. I think Russia is exerting this sort of influence each and every day.

Senator FISCHER. Could I follow up with just hopefully a short question? Is that okay, Senator Shaheen? Thank you.

Dr. Carpenter, when you mentioned that a NATO ally had basically had its borders breached so that one of its citizens was kidnapped and then you mentioned other countries that are not within NATO and events that are happening there, so does being a NATO member help these countries or—first of all, just yes or no. We do not have—I am already over my time. But would it be more helpful to say Estonia, the Baltics if American soldiers were stationed there?

Dr. CARPENTER. I think it absolutely does help. I think the article 5 guarantee deters Russia from doing a lot of things in the NATO space than it might otherwise want to do. That said, I do believe there is still room for some of this covert provocation and other types of operations that would be below the level of conflict, below the level of Crimea as well. Yes, United States force posture, in addition to the multinational battalions that are deployed in the Baltics, would augment that deterrent force.

Senator FISCHER. Thank you. Thank you, Madam Chair.

Thank you, Senator Shaheen.

Senator ERNST. Senator Shaheen.

Senator SHAHEEN. Thank you. Thank you, both Chair and Ranking Member, for holding this hearing.

Dr. Carpenter, I want to start with your recommendations that we need an independent investigation of Russia's meddling in our elections because I absolutely agree with you. I am puzzled by why we do not have more of the country outraged about this and why Congress is not outraged about this. This is not a partisan issue. This is about Russia meddling in our elections. That takes their activities in the United States on a political level, on espionage, whatever you talk—to a whole different level. They are not only doing it here, they are doing it in Europe. What message does it send to Russia that we have failed to take action in response to their activities?

Dr. CARPENTER. Well, I think it is incredibly provocative that we have thus far failed to seriously investigate this. I think we still have time to do so. But this was an influence operation aimed at the heart of American democracy, and if we do not respond, Russia will learn the lesson that it can continue to probe and it can continue to push the boundaries. It will interfere again, and it will continue to meddle in our process.

You know, there was an article that appeared in the Associated Press indicating that Mr. Manafort, who was campaign chairman, had proposed in fact confidential strategies, "that he would influence politics, business dealings, and news coverage inside the United States, Europe, and the former Soviet republics to benefit President Vladimir Putin's government". That is from an AP story. I cannot verify whether that is correct or not, but I can say if it
is correct, then we have a former campaign manager for our

President who was involved in the type of influence operation that we are discussing, the gray zone operation that we have been talking about in all these other countries here in the United States if this is true.

Senator SHAHEEN. Well, I agree.

Dr. Oliker, one of the things that you said I think in response to a question from Senator Peters was that Russia's actions in Crimea and Ukraine were not looked at as a provocation of the West. That really is very different than everything else I have heard in the Foreign Relations Committee and the Armed Services Committee about what Russia is doing. The explanations that I have heard in both of those committees from our witnesses has been that Putin is looking at how he can restore Russia's sphere of influence and how he can undermine the West, and he sees the United States as the best opportunity to do that. His actions are taken with that aim in mind. So do you disagree with that?

Dr. OLIKER. The way I would describe it is that Russia has been very unhappy with the security order that emerged at the end of the Cold War. If——

Senator SHAHEEN. Let me just interrupt you for a minute——

Dr. OLIKER. Yes.

Senator SHAHEEN.—because one of the things that I have heard from those people who were part of the effort with the fall of the Berlin Wall and the dissolution of the Soviet Union was that there were real efforts, outreach efforts made at a time when Vladimir Putin was working for Yeltsin to try and get Russia more engaged with the West, to try and point out that the expansion of NATO was not aimed at threatening Russia; it was aimed at protecting the West. So that does not square with what you are saying.

Dr. OLIKER. We have gone back and forth. Twenty-five years is a long time, and we have gone through phases of trying to engage the Russians and doing that less. The Russians, however, after a very brief period of indeed thinking that engagement was possible, began to view the United States as looking to limit and contain them, as they had in the past. Again, there have been times when Russian Governments, including Vladimir Putin's, have thought there was room for cooperation.

The problem has been that the Russian vision of cooperation is one of the quality of Russia and the United States as two great powers making decisions. The United States view has been of Russia as one more power that should certainly be at the table but not driving the decision-making. That fundamental disagreement has been I think at the core of the problem, that they expect far more than the United States has been able to give.

Senator SHAHEEN. General Cleveland, again, I could not agree more with what you are saying about efforts that we need to make to address the new threats that we are facing and that we have our military primarily designed to address conventional warfare. Testimony to that is that I have been on the Armed Services Committee now for over five years, and I never heard anybody talk about population-centric wars in those hearings.

You talked about changing military to address the new threats that we face, whether they be gray zone threats or cyber threats and that Congress would need to do that. Are there efforts within the military to make some of these changes? I ask you that—I asked a question about our ability to respond to what we are hearing from Russia in terms of, you know, that future warfare is one part conventional—four-to-one unconventional to conventional warfare. I did not get an answer that we have a strategy to address that. So are you seeing other places within our military where we ought to be looking to try and encourage a more robust response to the threats that we face today?

General CLEVELAND. I think, you know, part of the problem is that it is the old "if the only thing you have is a hammer, everything looks like a nail" sort of problem, right? We have defined what is war along what has been very convenient for us and where we were very successful.

Senator SHAHEEN. Right.

General CLEVELAND. The problem is our ability to dominate in that space—and I have written some articles about that that I have asked that they put in the record just in case you want to read some more about it, but our ability to dominate there by necessity has pushed folks into traditional forms where the weaker—and I put Russia in that basket as well—will use these techniques and have used these techniques since time immemorial against the stronger.

The problem and challenges that we have been able to—probably up through Vietnam—get away with using largely conventional forms of warfare against even population-centric wars with some success because you did not have a 24/7 news cycle, you did not have everybody with a smartphone sitting there as a reporter, and you did not have international bodies that actually start bringing people up on war crimes. Population control measures and things that you in the past would use or even the, you know, reduction of cities if you go back far enough, just no longer are acceptable.

There is a growing recognition that that aspect of our warfighting, that environment if you will, has shifted out from under us. There is discussion about, okay, what do we do about that. But it is like the 180-pound running back that gets the task of hitting, you know, the 290-pound defensive end, right? That 290-pound defensive end represents a pretty robust, you know, military-industrial complex, you know, to use Ike's term, that is kind of built to protect the Nation a certain way. That 180-pound running back cannot hit him shoulder pad to shoulder pad. You really have to go at the knees. In other words, there is something fundamentally—and that is where in my own way of thinking about this is we for too long have been kind of saying let us bounce these ideas off of conventional warfighting. That just has not worked, right?

My own analysis is I go to the more fundamental assumptions and ask myself whether those assumptions that built this military-industrial complex if you will are still valid. My answer is not completely, and that space that has changed is why I say that what is emerging is in fact this human domain of warfare where any domain, just like what was imposed with cyber, requires you to build—you know, have a concept in order to dominate there and build the right assets, you know, the concept, and then build the doctrine, the organization, the DOTMLPFs [Doctrine, Organization,

Training, Materiel, Leadership and Education, Personnel, Facilities and Policy] as the military terms it, in order to dominate there.

So there is awakening, I think, a growing understanding. I think there is reluctance because budgeting is a zero-some game, and if you say I am going to— you know, think about what happened with cyber. You created cyber as a top-down issue. All services have to cut out pieces of their budget to do what? Build a CYBERCOM and so forth.

So you are entering dangerous territory when you say, well, really what has happened in these wars, a domain of—the human domain has emerged because now your military campaign and the success of it depends on your ability to actually fight successfully in these population-centric wars. If you backwards engineer from that, you say, okay, well, then what does it take to fight there? What you bump up against is two philosophies. Either you need something new, which I would say 16 years after Afghanistan we probably ought to start asking that question, or you use differently what you have. I would say that is what we have been doing for this entire period.

I think that there is a growing understanding of it. Whether that understanding internally can lead to developing these new tools and taking more out of other people's budgets, I am skeptical of that. That is why I say—and I am not saying that, you know, it has got to be a lot, but, you know, I think if you look at Afghanistan and Iraq, I go back to my closing, you have to ask the question, you know, what would we have done differently? I have got to hope that it would be something different, right? Because we have not delivered on the political objectives that were set in force.

Senator SHAHEEN. Right. Thank you very much.

Madam Chair, could you share with the committee the articles that General Cleveland has submitted?

Senator ERNST. Absolutely. We will make sure those get to the committee members.

[The information referred to can be found in Appendix A.]

Senator ERNST. I think we have time if you would like just briefly a second round of questions. We will conclude with that second round.

Dr. Oliker, you note at the end of your written comments that you do not think a Crimea-like scenario is what we need to worry about in the future. As we witness continued gray zone activities from Russia throughout the Baltics and Balkans, I am worried about what scenario we might possibly see there in the future.

Specifically, I am concerned about Russia's involvement in Serbia right now and its impact on Iowa's sister country. We have a state partnership program with Kosovo, so I do get very concerned about those activities in Serbia and how they might lead to activities with Russia and Kosovo. So just last week, General Scaparrotti said he shared my concerns about Russia's activities in Serbia as well. So what type of Russia scenarios do you think we might see in the future specifically, you know, in that region?

Dr. OLIKER. I am also concerned about the Balkans, and I think they bear watching. I think the Russians are very much testing the waters for what is possible and what they can get away with. I think that—as I said, I do not think they went into Ukraine thinking that this was a way to get a standoff with United States, but they got one, and it has been more advantageous to them than they thought, and it has given them opportunities to push in other areas. I think very much the Balkans are one of them.

This said, one of the things I worry about most is not things that are intentional, you know, action response, but things that are unintentional. I worry a lot about Russian military provocations in the seas and the air of Europe. I worry about us operating in close proximity in Syria. I worry about things that could go wrong because there is so much distrust for very good reasons and because there—you know, there is a danger of overreaction on both sides.

So, you know, what I worry about most—I worry about what the Russians might do in the Balkans, but what I worry about most on the day-to-day level is that somebody is going to shoot down an airplane.

Senator ERNST. Right. Right. Those greater implications.

I thought it was interesting, Dr. Carpenter, that you mentioned the railcars that are being purchased with Russian dollars. That was brought to my attention by the Kosovars. They mentioned that there are railcars that have been purchased that are located in Serbia that have been run into Kosovo. So there are some concerns out there. They are wondering, you know, what is going on, what type of propaganda is this that exists out there. Do you have any brief comments on those types of activities?

Dr. CARPENTER. So earlier, I was referring to the railcars that Russia is using to conduct its Zapad exercise in Belarus, but in Serbia as well there were railcars that illegally tried to enter into the territory of Kosovo and that had come from Serbia.

I would say that Russian influence in Serbia is growing by the day. The pressure that Russia is exerting on the government in Belgrade is enormous. But I think almost more nefarious is the pressure and the ties that Russia has with Serbia's neighbor, particularly Republika Srpska within Bosnia and Herzegovina. There the ties between the Kremlin and Milorad Dodik, the President of Republika Srpska, are incredibly close, and Russia has essentially been supporting Dodik's efforts to talk about secession from the rest of Bosnia, which would be a disaster for the whole Balkans and can plunge the region into war yet again.

You have these active attempts by Russia in Bosnia, in Serbia, in Macedonia as well to undermine political structures and to use influence operations to penetrate government institutions, and it is all lubricated by corruption.

While the Serbian Government has been trying to find a way to pursue European Union integration, Russia has also come in and you have had the Russian Ambassador make comments in Belgrade about why is this in Serbia's interest?

Senator ERNST. Right.

Dr. CARPENTER. So clearly, they are fomenting opposition to Euro-Atlantic integration into Western norms and standards across the region.

Senator ERNST. Thank you very much.

Ranking Member Heinrich?

Senator HEINRICH. General Cleveland, I want to go back to something you mentioned in your testimony. You talked about potentially looking at something similar to section 1208 authority that we use in counterterrorism operations. Could you talk a little bit about, you know, what would it look like to have 1208 authority-like structure for gray zone entities that might be partnerable?

General CLEVELAND. Certainly. Again, I think 1208 and the strength of 1208 is in its ability to tap into SOCOM's very expedited processes to obtain equipment and to deploy forces in order to work with partners without having to go through the security—cooperation security assistance apparatus, right, which has done well by us I think for the most part. I think it needs some review overall and streamlining, but it is certainly not good enough for helping an advisor who goes into a country to say I need to build a CT force.

For instance, my own case in Paraguay, for instance, we did that and we used 1208, and you were able to get money invested. You bought equipment and weapons, and it was done through open contracts that SOCOM had, and they showed up with the counterparts fairly rapidly. If you go through the security assistance system, they have obviously a process in place to protect us from abuse and all that other kind of stuff. SOCOM has a process as well, but it is much more streamlined.

A 12XX program would do the same thing for countries that it is not necessarily a CT problem, but it is actually training forces in order to recognize, for instance, counterterrorism or unconventional warfare activities. It might be something that would have to be expanded to perhaps provide a country's police with some training as well. Its military perhaps would have to be competent in some elements of their own form of unconventional warfare, stay-behind activities if they are overrun, for example.

Senator HEINRICH. Right.

General CLEVELAND. As it exists right now, there is really not a pot of money that the soft forces can call upon to do that in what I think is the—with the agility that is necessary given the problem there.

Senator HEINRICH. Yes, I think that is something we may want to look at in the upcoming NDAA [National Defense Authorization Act] process as we move forward.

I want to go back to you, Dr. Carpenter, for one final thought and then I will relinquish the balance of my time. But, you know, it occurred to me that the recent Supreme Court decision around Citizens United has created a very different situation in our internal domestic elections than what has historically been the case. I have seen this in my own elections. I am sure all of my colleagues have watched as there has been less transparency as to where the money is actually coming from within elections.

In most national elections now you have a preponderance of the financing of advertisements and things within elections actually not originating with the candidates themselves. So you may have a Democrat and a Republican running for Congress someplace or running for the United States Senate, but the majority of the actual financial activity in that election is actually from third parties who it is not clear where the financing is coming from.

Do you see that fundamental lay of the land right now within our own election structure as an opening for Russia to be able to potentially manipulate, especially given their expertise at moving financial resources and networks?

Dr. CARPENTER. Absolutely, Senator. I think it is an eight-lane highway that allows Russia to plow financial resources into our electoral system. Russia has perfected this over the years. They do not use Russian Government institutions to funnel this money. They often use Russian oligarchs or not even oligarchs but businessmen who have ties to the Kremlin. These businessmen then funded NGOs or other types of organizations that are registered in the country where they want to have influence, and then those institutions in turn rely on shell companies and other types of organizations that are subsidiary to them to be able to fund money to candidates, to media organizations, to NGOs.

We saw spontaneously the emergence of NGOs, for example, in Romania that were anti-fracking that had come out of nowhere seemingly because Russia obviously had an interest in preventing that from happening due to its monopoly on gas flows to Western Europe.

So they are very adept at using all kinds of shell companies to funnel resources to political candidates and parties that suit their interests, not necessarily that are pro-Russian but in Europe that are euro-skeptic, that are either far right or far left, but that serve Russia's purpose in one way, shape, or form and advance their interests. And so, yes, Citizens United in my view has opened up floodgates for this type of money to pour into our system.

Senator HEINRICH. Thank you.

Senator ERNST. I want to thank our witnesses for joining us today for this subcommittee hearing. I appreciate your input, your thoughts. Ranking Member Heinrich, I appreciate your participation as well.

With that, we will close the subcommittee meeting on Emerging Threats and Capabilities. Thank you, witnesses.

[Whereupon, at 11:31 a.m., the hearing was adjourned.]

APPENDIX A

Unconventional Warfare in the Gray Zone

By Joseph L. Votel, Charles T. Cleveland, Charles T. Connett, and Will Irwin

n the months immediately following the terrorist attacks on the World Trade Center and Pentagon in the autumn of 2001, a small special operations forces (SOF) element and interagency team, supported by carrier- and land-based airstrikes, brought down the illegitimate Taliban government in Afghanistan that had been providing sanctuary for al Qaeda. This strikingly successful unconventional warfare (UW) operation was carried out with a U.S. "boots on the ground" presence of roughly 350 SOF and 110 interagency operatives working alongside an indigenous force of some 15,000 Afghan irregulars.[1] The Taliban regime fell within a matter of weeks. Many factors contributed to this extraordinary accomplishment, but its success clearly underscores the potential and viability of this form of warfare.

What followed this remarkably effective operation was more than a decade of challenging and costly large-scale irregular warfare campaigns in Afghanistan and Iraq employing hundreds of thousands

General Joseph L. Votel, USA, is the Commander of U.S. Special Operations Command. Lieutenant General Charles T. Cleveland, USA (Ret.), is a former Commander of U.S. Army Special Operations Command. Colonel Charles T. Connett, USA, is Director of the Commander's Initiatives Group at Headquarters U.S. Army Special Operations Command. Lieutenant Colonel Will Irwin, USA (Ret.), is a resident Senior Fellow at the Joint Special Operations University.

U.S. Air Force CV-22 Osprey's primary mission in 8th Special Operations Squadron is insertion, extraction, and resupply of unconventional warfare forces (U.S. Air Force/Jeremy T. Lock)

of U.S. and coalition troops. Now, as Operations *Enduring Freedom* and *Iraqi Freedom* have come to an end, the defense budget is shrinking, the Armed Forces are drawing down in strength, and support for further large-scale deployment of troops has ebbed. Our nation is entering a period where threats and our response to those threats will take place in a segment of the conflict continuum that some are calling the "Gray Zone,"[2] and SOF are the preeminent force of choice in such conditions.

The Gray Zone is characterized by intense political, economic, informational, and military competition more fervent in nature than normal steady-state diplomacy, yet short of conventional war. It is hardly new, however. The Cold War was a 45-year-long Gray Zone struggle in which the West succeeded in checking the spread of communism and ultimately witnessed the dissolution of the Soviet Union. To avoid superpower confrontations that might escalate to all-out nuclear war, the Cold War was largely a proxy war, with the United States and Soviet Union backing various state or nonstate actors in small regional conflicts and executing discrete superpower intervention and counter-intervention around the globe. Even the Korean and Vietnam conflicts were fought under political

constraints that made complete U.S. or allied victory virtually impossible for fear of escalation.

After more than a decade of intense large-scale counterinsurgency and counterterrorism campaigning, the U.S. capability to conduct Gray Zone operations—small-footprint, low-visibility operations often of a covert or clandestine nature—may have atrophied. In the words of one writer, the United States must recognize that "the space between war and peace is not an empty one"[3] that we can afford to vacate. Because most of our current adversaries choose to engage us in an asymmetrical manner, this represents an area where "America's enemies and adversaries prefer to operate."[4]

Nations such as Russia, China, and Iran have demonstrated a finely tuned risk calculus. Russia belligerently works to expand its sphere of influence and control into former Soviet or Warsaw Pact territory to the greatest degree possible without triggering a North Atlantic Treaty Organization Article 5 response. China knows that its assertive actions aimed at expanding its sovereignty in the South China Sea fall short of eliciting a belligerent U.S. or allied response. Iran has displayed an impressive degree of sophistication in its ability to employ an array of proxies against U.S. and Western interests.

While "Gray Zone" refers to a space in the peace-conflict continuum, the methods for engaging our adversaries in that environment have much in common with the political warfare that was predominant during the Cold War years. Political warfare is played out in that space between diplomacy and open warfare, where traditional statecraft is inadequate or ineffective and large-scale conventional military options are not suitable or are deemed inappropriate for a variety of reasons. Political warfare is a population-centric engagement that seeks to influence, to persuade, even to co-opt. One of its staunchest proponents, George Kennan, described it as "the employment of all the means at a nation's command, short of war, to achieve its national objectives," including overt measures such as white propaganda, political alliances, and economic programs, to "such covert operations as clandestine support of 'friendly' foreign elements, 'black' psychological warfare, and even encouragement of underground resistance in hostile states."[5]

Organized political warfare served as the basis for U.S. foreign policy during the early Cold War years and it was later revived during the Reagan administration. But, as Max Boot of the Council on Foreign Relations observed, it has become a lost art and one that he and others believe needs to be rediscovered and mastered.[6] SOF are optimized for providing the preeminent military contribution to a national political warfare capability because of their inherent proficiency in low-visibility, small-footprint, and politically sensitive operations. SOF provide national decisionmakers "strategic options for protecting and advancing U.S. national interests without committing major combat forces to costly, long-term contingency operations."[7]

Human Domain-Centric Core Tasks for SOF

SOF provide several options for operating in the political warfare realm, especially those core tasks that are grouped under the term *special warfare*. Foreign internal defense (FID) operations are conducted to support a friendly foreign government in its efforts to defeat an internal threat. In terms of strategic application, UW represents the opposite approach, where the U.S. Government supports a resistance movement or insurgency against an occupying power or adversary government.

Both of these special warfare tasks rely heavily on SOF ability to build trust and confidence with our indigenous partners—host nation military and paramilitary forces in the case of FID, irregular resistance elements in the case of UW—to generate mass through indigenous forces, thus eliminating the need for a large U.S. force presence (see figure 1). It is this indigenous mass that helps minimize strategic risk during Gray Zone operations: "Special Warfare campaigns stabilize or destabilize a regime by operating 'through and with' local state or nonstate partners, rather than through unilateral U.S. action."[8] As described in a recent RAND study, discrete and usually multi-year special warfare campaigns are characterized by six central features:

- Their goal is stabilizing or destabilizing the targeted regime.
- Local partners provide the main effort.
- U.S. forces maintain a small (or no) footprint in the country.
- They are typically of long duration and may require extensive preparatory work better measured in months (or years) than days.
- They require intensive interagency cooperation; Department of Defense (DOD) elements may be subordinate to the Department of State or the Central Intelligence Agency.
- They employ "political warfare" methods to mobilize, neutralize, or integrate individuals or groups from the tactical to strategic levels.[9]

Many examples exist of successful long-duration, low-visibility U.S. SOF-centric FID operations in Latin America, Asia, and Africa. From 1980 through 1991, U.S. support to the government of El Salvador fighting an insurgency in that country included an advisory force that never exceeded 55 personnel. The conflict ended with a favorable negotiated

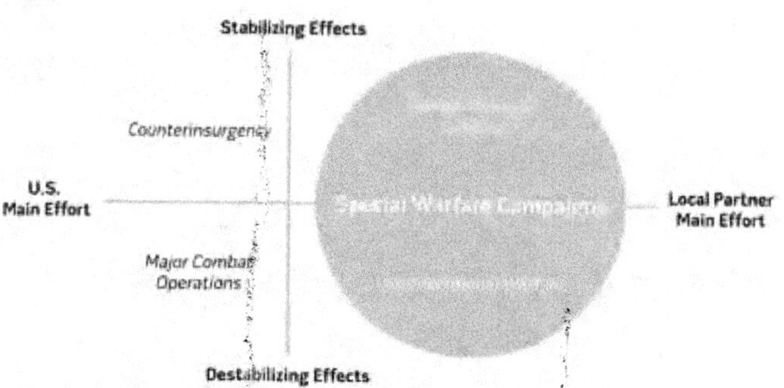

Figure 1.

settlement. Similar successes against lower level insurgencies took place in neighboring Honduras and Guatemala. More recently, U.S. SOF have played a central role in effective long-term FID efforts conducted in support of the governments of Colombia and the Philippines.

Less well known and understood by those outside of SOF is the core task of unconventional warfare.

Doctrine

This year marks the release of the first joint U.S. doctrine publication for the planning, execution, and assessment of UW operations.[10] The United States has been producing UW doctrine since the first series of field manuals published from 1943 to 1944 by the wartime Office of Strategic Services (OSS). However, for the past seven decades, that doctrine has been produced by the U.S. Army. Despite the longstanding recognition in Army doctrine that UW is inherently joint and interagency in character, single-Service doctrine is at a disadvantage in reaching joint and interagency audiences. Therefore, a joint UW publication was needed.

Army Special Forces remain the only element in the U.S. Armed Forces organized, trained, and equipped specifically for UW. However, while Special Forces continue to play a central role in the mission, Joint Publication 3-05.1, *Unconventional Warfare*, recognizes the roles of other SOF, as well as important supporting functions of conventional forces. It also provides insight into the

importance of interagency planning, coordination, and collaboration; other U.S. Government departments and agencies are not only frequently involved, but they are also often in the lead.

Unconventional warfare is fundamentally an indirect application of U.S. power, one that leverages foreign population groups to maintain or advance U.S. interests. It is a highly discretionary form of warfare that is most often conducted clandestinely, and because it is also typically conducted covertly, at least initially, it nearly always has a strong interagency element. It can be subtle or it can be aggressive. The U.S.-indigenous irregular benefactor-proxy relationship, if successful, achieves mutually beneficial objectives (although there can also be divergent interests between benefactor and proxy).

Advocates of UW first recognize that, among a population of self-determination seekers, human interest in liberty trumps loyalty to a self-serving dictatorship, that those who aspire to freedom can succeed in deposing corrupt or authoritarian rulers, and that unfortunate population groups can and often do seek alternatives to a life of fear, oppression, and injustice. Second, advocates believe that there is a valid role for the U.S. Government in encouraging and empowering these freedom seekers when doing so helps to secure U.S. national security interests.

Historically, the U.S. military has conducted UW primarily in wartime to assist indigenous resistance movements in defeating or causing the withdrawal of a foreign occupation force. In peacetime,

UW can take the form of covert paramilitary operations conducted by other agencies of the U.S. Government or clandestine military operations. Through diplomacy, development, and other means, other government departments and agencies, such as the Department of State and U.S. Agency for International Development (USAID), can help shape the environment or provide support to resistance in other ways. When Congress passed the Boland Amendment during the 1980s, halting all but humanitarian U.S. aid to the Contras, USAID became the leading provider of support to the Nicaraguan resistance.

If a resistance movement or insurgency exists within a country whose government threatens U.S. security interests, the movement asks for assistance from the United States, and the group's operational methods and behavior are deemed to be acceptable by the U.S. Government, the President of the United States might approve initiation of UW operations. The target government could be a state sponsor of terrorism or a proliferator of weapons of mass destruction technology. It might be a government engaged in ethnic cleansing or other crimes against humanity, or a state that willingly allows transit or provides sanctuary or other forms of support to terrorists. Or it could be a state that actively and aggressively, even belligerently, takes action to expand its territorial sovereignty with the result of undermining regional stability.

Under certain circumstances, the prudent employment of coercive force, by empowering an indigenous opposition element, can force a target government to do something it might not otherwise be inclined to do. Under other conditions, the goal could be simply to disrupt certain operations or activities of the hostile government, such as interfering with proliferation actions, safeguarding a population group targeted for genocide by the incumbent regime, or imposing extraordinary and unexpected difficulties in consolidating the occupation of a country that has been invaded, thus altering the adversary state's cost and risk calculus.

This was the case during the prolonged U.S. UW campaign in support of Tibetan resistance fighters against Chinese occupiers from 1957 to 1969, and again with the UW operation in support of the Mujahideen in Afghanistan in their struggle against the Soviet 40th Army after its invasion and occupation of that country. During the second Reagan administration, however, the objective of the Afghanistan mission changed from a cost-imposing strategy to forcing the withdrawal of Soviet forces from the country. The success of that mission had enormous political and historical ramifications, beginning a chain of events that eventually resulted in the collapse of the Soviet Union and an end to the Cold War.

In some cases, UW can be used as a regime change mechanism, enabling an indigenous resistance or insurgent group to overthrow the existing government. In a wartime supporting role, UW operations can be a shaping effort in support of larger, conventional force operations, such as the very successful UW operations executed by U.S. SOF with Kurdish Peshmerga forces in northern Iraq during the 2003 invasion of that country. Alternatively, it could be the main effort in a military campaign, as was the UW operation that brought down the Afghan Taliban regime in 2001.

Unconventional warfare has often been the option of choice in situations where the President (or a theater commander in wartime) wishes to initiate operations much sooner than could be accomplished with the mobilization, preparation, and deployment of conventional forces. Such was the case with the operation by the 5th Special Forces Group (Airborne) and Air Force Special Tactics operators in Afghanistan in 2001.

A requirement might exist for operations in areas not easily accessible to conventional forces or that lend themselves to UW in an economy of force role in secondary theaters of war. Circumstances such as this resulted in several UW operations during World War II, including those in Yugoslavia, Albania, Greece, northern Italy, Norway, Burma, Thailand, Indochina, and China. In conducting such operations, U.S.

forces will typically support three main elements of the resistance movement or insurgency—the underground, auxiliary, and guerrilla force. The underground is a cellular-based organization that operates in urban or other areas usually inaccessible to the guerrilla force. Composed of part-time volunteers, the auxiliary component clandestinely provides a wide range of support to both the underground and guerrillas. Probably the most familiar element is the guerrilla force, an organization of irregular combatants who comprise the armed or overt military component of the resistance.

Often the resistance includes a shadow government within the country capable of performing government functions on behalf of the movement. There might also be a government-in-exile in another country—often as a result of being displaced by an invading and occupying power—which remains the internationally recognized government of the occupied state. Nearly all the countries of Western Europe overrun and occupied by German forces in World War II established governments-in-exile in London.

Methods used by the resistance in meeting its objectives could include subversive activities such as mass protests, work slowdowns or stoppages, boycotts, infiltration of government offices, and the formation of front groups. These activities are primarily aimed at undermining the military, economic, psychological, or political strength or morale of the government or occupation authority.

Sabotage can be a means of physically damaging the government's military or industrial production facilities, economic resources, or other targets. During World War II, sabotage targets for Allied SOF included road and rail lines of communication, hydroelectric power production and distribution facilities, telecommunications facilities, canal locks, radar sites, port facilities, factories engaged in the manufacture of war materiel, and military supply dumps or other targets.

Guerrilla warfare operations are carried out against military or other security forces to reduce their effectiveness and negatively impact the enemy's morale.

Jedburghs get instructions from briefing officer in London, 1944 (U.S. Office of Strategic Services)

Allied-supported World War II guerrilla operations in occupied France, Belgium, and Holland, as well as those in the Philippines, were instrumental in facilitating Allied ground campaigns.

Many types of information activities are used to influence friendly, adversary, and neutral audiences. Resistance groups craft narratives that best convey the movement's purpose and leverage key grievances of importance to the people. Another important purpose of information operations could be to encourage disparate resistance factions to work together to achieve common objectives.

Because the FID and UW core tasks are so closely related, employing many similar capabilities, a comprehensive Gray Zone special warfare campaign could include aspects of both missions, thus capitalizing on their synergistic effect. Among the U.S. objectives in initiating support to the Nicaraguan resistance in the early 1980s, for example, was to aid the U.S. FID program in El Salvador by pressuring the Nicaraguan Sandinista government to halt its support to the Salvadoran Farabundo Marti National Liberation Front.[11]

Today, "regional powers such as Russia, China, India, Indonesia, Brazil, Nigeria, South Africa, Turkey, and Iran assert growing power and influence. . . . Sub-state actors (e.g., clans, tribes, ethnic and religious minorities) seek greater autonomy from the central government."[12]

The complex nature of the future operating environment will often render traditional applications of the diplomatic and economic instruments ineffective or inappropriate. Decisionmakers might wish to avoid the political risks and consequences, including escalation and mission creep, associated with direct military engagement. At such times, UW might be the only viable option through which the U.S. Government can indirectly achieve political objectives. By supporting indigenous insurgencies, resistance movements, or other internal opposition groups, the U.S. Government can employ UW as a strategic tool of coercion, disruption, or to lead to the defeat of a hostile regime.

An Enigmatic History

U.S. UW doctrine has evolved from its World War II roots when the Allies conducted UW in at least 18 countries worldwide. Operations by U.S. forces include a highly successful UW campaign in an "economy of force" role in Burma and operations by stay-behind guerrilla leaders in the Philippines, where UW proved invaluable to U.S. land forces during the liberation of that country. Probably the best prepared UW operations were conducted in the European theater, where Allied SOF benefited from an extensive and well-tested UW command and sustainment infrastructure, to say nothing of state-of-the-art training and equipment.

On May 25, 1940, when the German defeat of France seemed all but inevitable, the British Chiefs of Staff met to consider possible courses of action. Once France fell, they believed, Britain's only hope lie in rescue by the as yet immobilized United States. Until that time, "the best hope would lie in subversion, to rot the enemy-held countries from within."[13] Prime Minister Winston Churchill, who saw great value in helping the people of occupied Europe to play an active part in their own liberation, signed the charter for the Special Operations Executive (SOE) in July 1940.

Four years later, Special Force Headquarters, an Allied UW command subordinate to General Dwight D. Eisenhower's theater command and staffed by the British SOE and the U.S. OSS, along with Free French and other Allied personnel, deployed several types of special forces into denied territory in occupied Europe. Among the better known units were the multinational Jedburgh teams. Deployed in support of the French Resistance, "Jed" teams were primarily assigned the dual mission of organizing, equipping, training, and advising guerrilla forces; and serving as a communication link between the Resistance and the Allied high command in London. But they served an additional purpose that was just as important, though seldom mentioned and largely unheralded.

Many Jedburgh veterans later testified that they spent much of their time preventing the various resistance factions—each with different postwar political agendas and often violently opposed to one another—from fighting each other and keeping them focused on the common enemy, the German occupiers.[14] One need look no further than Syria today to imagine how much more difficult the Allied ground campaign to liberate France might have been had this internecine rivalry not been held in check. With all of their tactical and operational successes, the Jedburghs' greatest strategic contribution might have been in keeping the tenuous French Forces of the Interior coalition intact, making the Jeds truly warrior-diplomats. Eisenhower later wrote of the work of the Jedburghs and other SOE and OSS special forces: "In no previous war, and in no other theater during this war, have resistance forces been so closely harnessed to the main military effort."[15]

Unconventional warfare continued to play a significant role in U.S. foreign policy during the early Cold War years, often in the form of covert paramilitary operations led by the Central Intelligence Agency. Military UW conducted during the Korean War was only minimally effective, primarily because of a lack of training and experience on the part of those charged with executing it.

In April 1961, President John F. Kennedy had to weather the politically embarrassing failure of the ill-advised Bay of Pigs affair in Cuba. Secretly working at a military base in Guatemala under the guise of a mission to train Guatemalan forces, U.S. Army Special Forces trained the rebel force of Cuban exiles in small unit guerrilla warfare operations.[16] Unfortunately, those forces were then employed in an inappropriate manner, attempting a conventional amphibious landing and beach assault against superior forces.

Throughout the Cold War, many hard lessons were learned in places as wide-ranging as Eastern Europe, China, Indonesia, Tibet, North Vietnam, Nicaragua, and elsewhere. One major success came during the 1980s with support provided to the Afghan Mujahideen that resulted in expulsion of Soviet occupation forces from that country.

The post–Cold War era brought two major UW successes for U.S. forces. First came the operation to oust the Taliban regime in Afghanistan in late 2001, described at the beginning of this article. The second was the UW operation in northern Iraq that contributed to victory during the 2003 U.S. invasion of that country.

Civil Resistance

Today's joint UW doctrine recognizes variances of resistance that span the breadth of organized opposition from reform-oriented social movements[17] to social revolution,[18] to insurgency, and on to larger armed revolutionary movements.

Recently, there has been growing interest in UW operations that leverage existing social movements and nonviolent, civil resistance–based social revolution. Contributing to this interest is the favorable track record of such movements in comparison with armed resistance. Based on one recent study of 323 resistance movements whose objective was regime change or expulsion of a foreign occupation force between 1900 and 2006, those movements following a strategy of "nonviolent resistance against authoritarian regimes were twice as likely to succeed as violent movements."[19]

The main reason for this is that movements choosing to follow a nonviolent strategy attract a much larger domestic support base than armed and violent movements. While even the most successful of the armed variety hope to attract a support base numbering in the tens of thousands, supporters numbering in the hundreds of thousands for nonviolent resistance campaigns are not unusual. Moreover, nonviolent movements find it much easier to garner backing from the international community, so important in building coalition UW support.

Figure 2 (created by the Naval Postgraduate School's Doowan Lee) illustrates the relationship between social movements, social revolution, and unconventional warfare. An example of the scenario depicted by sector G at the center of the diagram can be seen in U.S. support provided to resistance elements during Serbia's "Bulldozer Revolution" that resulted in the overthrow of dictator Slobodan Milosevic, then president of what remained of Yugoslavia.

When massive demonstrations in September 1999 demanded Milosevic's resignation, he responded with a brutal crackdown by police and the army. One opposition group, however, remained determined to oust Milosevic through a campaign of nonviolent civil disobedience. *Otpor* (Serbian for resistance), an underground Serbian youth movement formed in 1998 by a dozen college students, eventually grew to a nationwide grassroots popular movement claiming a membership of more than 70,000.[20] The Bill Clinton administration decided to support the movement and provided much in the form of funding, computers, and political and military advice.

The domestic anti-Milosevic campaign culminated in October 2000 with a nationwide general strike and a march on the capital by hundreds of thousands of protesters from across the country. Milosevic finally announced his resignation the following day, bringing to an end a brutal 13-year regime.

For several reasons, SOF are ideally suited to contribute to U.S. support to such social revolutions. First and foremost, it must be remembered that just because a movement opts to follow a nonviolent strategy is no guarantee that the revolution will remain nonviolent. Several of the Arab Spring revolutions have shown that such movements must be prepared in the event that severe government repressive measures drive them to abandon the nonviolent strategy and resort to an armed resistance campaign rather than forfeiting their cause. In fact, in the case of Serbia's Bulldozer Revolution, some elements of the resistance were prepared to do just that had it become necessary.

Participants at a recent UW/ Resistance seminar (co-sponsored by U.S. Special Operations Command Europe and Joint Special Operations University) at the Baltic Defence College in Estonia observed that, based on the experiences of some former Warsaw Pact nations in their civil resistance–based post–Cold War revolutions, "resistance

Figure 2.

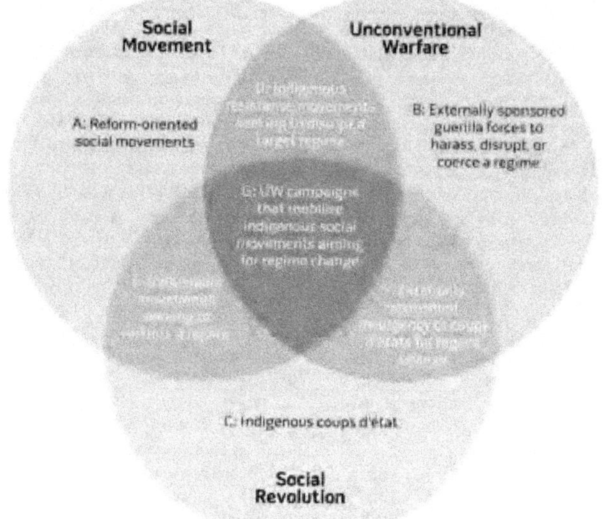

can be armed or non-violent, but both must be planned for."[21]

Clearly, SOF have a traditional UW role in providing the necessary organizing, equipping, training, and advising functions to support such an armed resistance effort, but this role can have a much greater chance of succeeding if SOF are involved as advisors early on, during the nonviolent resistance campaign. Whether early U.S. support is covert or overt, if it reaches the point where lead-agency responsibility transfers from the Department of State or another government agency to DOD, early involvement by SOF can ensure that such a transfer is smooth and is executed at full speed, much like the passing of a baton in a relay race, rather than a dangerous and counterproductive stop-and-go affair. SOF capabilities and expertise transcend lead-agency boundaries.

An early decision to support a movement can also pay dividends, providing the opportunity for SOF or other U.S. Government departments or agencies to influence, shape, and steer the movement; encourage and facilitate the consolidation or alliance of competing but compatible factions; or thwart or inhibit the development of competing factions or movements that are incompatible and adversarial.

DOTMLPF Implications

Much is already being done toward developing or upgrading joint and Service UW-related doctrine, and better organizing and preparing our primary UW force. While some doctrine, organization, training, materiel, leader development, personnel, and facilities (DOTMLPF) requirements have been identified and solutions determined, full implications should continue to emerge through a rigorous and disciplined requirements assessment process.

In recognizing a need for doctrine updating, one Theater Special Operations Command commander recently observed:

The conditions of 2014 are different than those of 1944, and the tools with which unconventional warfare is waged today differ greatly. We must advance from the nostalgic vision of remote guerrilla bases in denied territory and adapt to a world of split-second communications and data transfer, non-violent resistance, cyber and economic warfare, and the manipulation of international law to undermine national sovereignty. . . . In our era, unconventional warfare is more likely to take the form of a civil resistance movement, perhaps manipulated by foreign powers, that seeks to provoke a violent government response in order to destroy that government's legitimacy in the eyes of the international community. Waging and countering this new unconventional warfare demands great sophistication and agility.[22]

Implementation of emerging UW concepts and doctrine requires persistent, low-visibility presence around the world and the development of a network of useful and influential contacts. Foreign internal defense, security assistance, foreign officer exchange programs, foreign education and study opportunities, and special assignments are important means of contributing to this.

To meet the challenges of UW support to social movements or social revolution, a deeper understanding of the dynamics of civil resistance and how UW can be conducted through such subversive (and often nonviolent) movements is required. Understanding conditions where more violent methods might be problematic, if not counterproductive, calls for an in-depth understanding of the theories, concepts, and methods associated with social movement influence, mobilization, and activism. SOF must continually work to upgrade their training regimen and education curriculum in areas such as:

- social movement theory
- regional history, cultural studies, and language proficiency
- creation and preparation of an underground
- cyber UW tools and methods
- influence operations
- negotiation and mediation skills
- popular mobilization dynamics
- subversion and political warfare
- social network analysis and sociocultural analysis.

To make a thorough assessment of a group and to be in a position to capitalize on the advantages of early observation and possible engagement, SOF should be capable of recognizing the conditions and early indicators of resistance.

Materiel requirements are such that they apply to other SOF core tasks as well as UW. Senior leaders have long recognized that SOF require improvements in denied area penetration and standoff capabilities and an ability to perform critical core tasks for extended periods in high-risk situations.[23] The requirement for low-visibility and stealthy air platforms might not be limited to infiltration, exfiltration, and personnel recovery. Modified versions of these platforms could serve as tankers or gunships, or platforms for information operations, aerial resupply, precision strike, and terminal guidance.

Materiel requirements might also include a stealthy, long-endurance SOF drone with global surveillance and strike capability. Other payloads could provide the capability to disseminate electronic messages via radio or television broadcast, in standoff mode, to target audiences in denied areas. Unmanned aerial systems might also have the ability to emplace remote unattended ground sensors capable of detecting, classifying, and determining the direction of movement of personnel, wheeled vehicles, and tracked vehicles.

A Critical Policy Gap

After a few early political warfare successes in the 1950s, along with some clear failures, President Eisenhower once considered appointing a National Security Council (NSC)-level "director of unconventional or non-military warfare," with responsibilities including such areas as "economic warfare, psychological warfare, political warfare, and foreign information."[24] In other words, he saw the need for an NSC-level director of political warfare, someone to quarterback the habitually interagency effort. This need still exists to achieve unity of effort across all aspects of national power (diplomatic, informational, military, and economic) across the continuum of international competition. As Max Boot has observed, political warfare has become a lost art which no department or agency of the U.S. Government views as a core mission.[25]

Conclusion

Unconventional warfare, whether conducted by the United States or Russia or any other state seeking to advance national interests through Gray Zone proxy warfare, has a rich history but continues to evolve to meet changing global conditions. One certainty in a world of continuing disorder, a world bereft of Cold War clarity and relative "stability," where globalization has enabled almost continuous change, is that the UW mission must continue to adapt and so must those responsible for executing it.

U.S. forces can likely have the greatest chance for success in Gray Zone UW operations when engaged early in a resistance movement's development and continuously thereafter. As demonstrated in the U.S. operation to support Afghanistan's Northern Alliance in 2001, however, it can also succeed with relatively mature and experienced resistance groups, when a benefactor state's support might be just enough to tip the scales in favor of a movement that has been largely stalemated.

One remaining requirement is that of determining what Gray Zone UW success looks like and establishing meaningful criteria for measuring the effectiveness of such operations. The very concept of "winning" must be fundamentally reexamined in the context of a future environment where we will likely not commit large military formations in decisive engagements against similarly armed foes.

A Gray Zone "win" is not a win in the classic warfare sense. Winning is perhaps better described as maintaining the U.S. Government's positional advantage, namely the ability to influence partners, populations, and threats toward achievement of our regional or strategic objectives. Specifically, this will mean retaining decision space, maximizing desirable strategic options, or simply denying an adversary a decisive positional advantage.

In these human-centric struggles, our successes cannot be solely our own in that they must be largely defined and accomplished by our indigenous friends and coalition partners as they realize respectively acceptable political outcomes. Successful culmination of Gray Zone conflicts will not be marked by pomp and ceremony, but rather should, ideally, pass with little or no fanfare or indication of our degree of involvement.

History has shown that no two UW situations or solutions are identical, thus rendering cookie-cutter responses not only meaningless but also often counterproductive. Planners and operators most in demand in this difficult task will be those capable of thinking critically and creatively, warriors unhindered by the need for continuous and detailed guidance. Such special operators will be most capable of performing critical UW tasks under politically sensitive conditions, ensuring that they can serve, in the tradition of their Jedburgh predecessors, as true warrior-diplomats. JFQ

Notes

[1] Doug Stanton, *Horse Soldiers: The Extraordinary Story of a Band of U.S. Soldiers Who Rode to Victory in Afghanistan* (New York: Scribner, 2009), 347; and George Tenet, with Bill Harlow, *At the Center of the Storm: My Years at the CIA* (New York: HarperCollins Publishers, 2007), 225.

[2] See, for example, General Joseph L. Votel, statement before the House Armed Services Committee Subcommittee on Emerging Threats and Capabilities, March 18, 2015; Captain Philip Kapusta, U.S. Special Operations Command (USSOCOM) white paper, "Defining Gray Zone Challenges," April 2015; David Barno and Nora Bensahel, "Fighting and Winning in the 'Gray Zone,'" *War on the Rocks*, May 2015; and Nobuhiro Kubo, Linda Sieg, and Phil Stewart, "Japan, U.S. Differ on China in Talks on 'Gray Zone' Military Threats," Reuters, March 10, 2014.

[3] Nadia Schadlow, "Peace and War: The Space Between," *War on the Rocks*, August 2014, available at <http://warontherocks.com/2014/08/peace-and-war-the-space-between/>.

[4] Ibid.

[5] George F. Kennan, "Policy Planning Staff Memorandum," May 4, 1948, National Archives, RG 273, Records of the National Security Council, NSC 10/2, available at <http://academic.brooklyn.cuny.edu/history/johnson/65ciafounding3.htm>.

[6] Max Boot and Michael Doran, Council on Foreign Relations Policy Innovation Memorandum No. 33, *Political Warfare* (Washington, DC: Council on Foreign Relations, June 7, 2013).

[7] USSOCOM, *Special Operations Forces Operating Concept*, May 2013, 1.

[8] Dan Madden et al., *Special Warfare: The Missing Middle in U.S. Coercive Options* (Santa Monica, CA: RAND, 2014), 1.

[9] Ibid., 2.

[10] Joint Publication (JP) 1-02, *Department of Defense Dictionary of Military and Associated Terms* (Washington, DC: The Joint Staff, November 8, 2010, as amended through October 15, 2015), defines *unconventional warfare* as "activities conducted to enable a resistance movement or insurgency to coerce, disrupt, or overthrow a government or occupying power by operating through or with an underground, auxiliary, and guerrilla force in a denied area."

[11] David Ronfeldt and Brian Jenkins, *The Nicaraguan Resistance and U.S. Policy* (Santa Monica, CA: RAND, 1989), 15.

[12] USSOCOM, *SOF Operating Concept*, 2.

[13] William Mackenzie, *The Secret History of S.O.E.: Special Operations Executive, 1940–1945* (London: St. Ermin's Press, 2000), xix.

[14] Will Irwin, *The Jedburghs: The Secret History of the Allied Special Forces, France 1944* (New York: PublicAffairs, 2005), 236, based on correspondence and interviews with more than 60 U.S., British, and French Jedburgh veterans from 1985 to 2005.

[15] General Dwight D. Eisenhower, letters to the executive director of SOE and to the director of the Office of Strategic Services London, May 31, 1945. See Irwin, xxii, 280.

[16] Central Intelligence Agency History Staff, *Official History of the Bay of Pigs Operation*, Vol. 2: *Participation in the Conduct of Foreign Policy*, October 1979 (declassified July 25, 2011), 57–98.

[17] JP 3-05.1, *Joint Special Operations Task Force Operations* (Washington, DC: The Joint Staff, April 26, 2007), defines *social movement* as "a collective challenge by people with common purposes and solidarity in sustained interactions with elites, opponents, and authorities."

[18] JP 3-05.1 defines *social revolution* as "a rapid transformation of a society's state and class structures, accompanied and in part accomplished through popular revolts."

[19] Erica Chenoweth and Maria J. Stephan, "Drop Your Weapons: When and Why Civil Resistance Works," *Foreign Affairs* 93, no. 4 (July/August 2014), 94–106.

[20] Roger Cohen, "Who Really Brought Down Milosevic?" *New York Times Magazine*, November 26, 2000, available at <www.nytimes.com/2000/11/26/magazine/who-really-brought-down-milosevic.html>.

[21] U.S. Special Operations Command Europe (USSOCEUR) and Joint Special Operations University (JSOU), "Unconventional Warfare/Resistance Seminar Series After Action Report," November 2014, 3.

[22] USSOCEUR, "Sponsor Welcoming Remarks Prepared for COMSOCEUR," JSOU/BALTDEFCOL/SOCEUR Unconventional Warfare Seminar, Tartu, Estonia, November 4–6, 2014.

[23] See General Bryan D. Brown, then Deputy Commander, USSOCOM, testimony before the Senate Committee on Armed Services Subcommittee on Emerging Threats and Capabilities on the State of Special Operations Forces, April 9, 2003, 12; and Michael G. Vickers, "Transforming U.S. Special Operations Forces," Center for Strategic and Budgetary Assessments, prepared for OSD Net Assessment, August 2005, 11.

[24] National Security Council memorandum, "Discussion at the 209th Meeting of the National Security Council, Thursday, August 5, 1954," August 6, 1954; Eisenhower Presidential Library; Papers as President (Ann Whitman File), NSC Series, Box 5.

[25] Boot and Doran.

UNITED STATES
SPECIAL OPERATIONS COMMAND

White Paper

The Gray Zone

9 September 2015

Defining Gray Zone Challenges

Gray zone security challenges, existing short of a formal state of war, present novel complications for U.S. policy and interests in the 21st century. We have well-developed vocabularies, doctrines and mental models to describe war and peace, but the numerous gray zone challenges in between defy easy categorization. For purposes of this paper, gray zone challenges are defined as *competitive interactions among and within state and non-state actors that fall between the traditional war and peace duality.* They are characterized by ambiguity about the nature of the conflict, opacity of the parties involved, or uncertainty about the relevant policy and legal frameworks.

Gray zone challenges can be understood as a pooling of diverse conflicts exhibiting common characteristics. Notably, combining these challenges does not imply a single solution, since each situation contains unique actors and aspects. Overall, gray zone challenges rise above normal, everyday peacetime geo-political competition and are *aggressive, perspective-dependent, and ambiguous.*

As the world's leading superpower and *de facto* guarantor of the current world order, American national security interests span the globe and intersect with numerous circumstances fitting the definition of gray zone challenges. However, many of these challenges exist independent of U.S. agency or action and do not merit American involvement (e.g. civil conflicts in Africa). Accordingly, this paper acknowledges and briefly discusses the larger construct of gray zone challenges across the world, but it focuses on the United States' national security interests and those gray zone challenges such as Russian actions in eastern Ukraine and Daesh (ISIS) that are relevant to America today.

Gray Zone Challenges – The new and old normal

The U.S. government can improve its ability to operate effectively in the gray zone between war and peace by reshaping its intellectual, organizational and institutional models. America's conventional military dominance and status as a global power guarantee continual challenges and incentivize competitors to oppose the United States in ways designed to nullify our military advantage. The U.S. already possesses the right mix of tools to prevail in the gray zone, but it must think, organize, and act differently.

Gray zone challenges are not new. Monikers such as irregular warfare, low-intensity conflict, asymmetric warfare, Military Operations Other Than War (MOOTW), and Small Wars have all been employed to describe this phenomenon in the past. President Kennedy was speaking about the gray zone during his 1962 address to West Point's graduating class when he said:

> This is another type of war, new in its intensity, ancient in its origin—war by guerrillas, subversives, insurgents, assassins, war by ambush instead of by combat; by infiltration, instead of aggression, seeking victory by eroding and exhausting the enemy instead of engaging him.[1]

Massive investments in technology and unrivaled expertise in combined arms warfare give the U.S. a conventional military dominance not seen since the Roman Empire. However, this only holds true for the model of state-on-state conflicts dominated by traditional militaries fighting one another for battlefield supremacy. History shows this depiction of war is accurate only by exception.

---

[1] John F. Kennedy: "Remarks at West Point to the Graduating Class of the U.S. Military Academy." June 6, 1962. Online by Gerhard Peters and John T. Woolley, *The American Presidency Project.* http://www.presidency.ucsb.edu/ws/?pid=8695.

A Century of War and Gray Zone Challenges

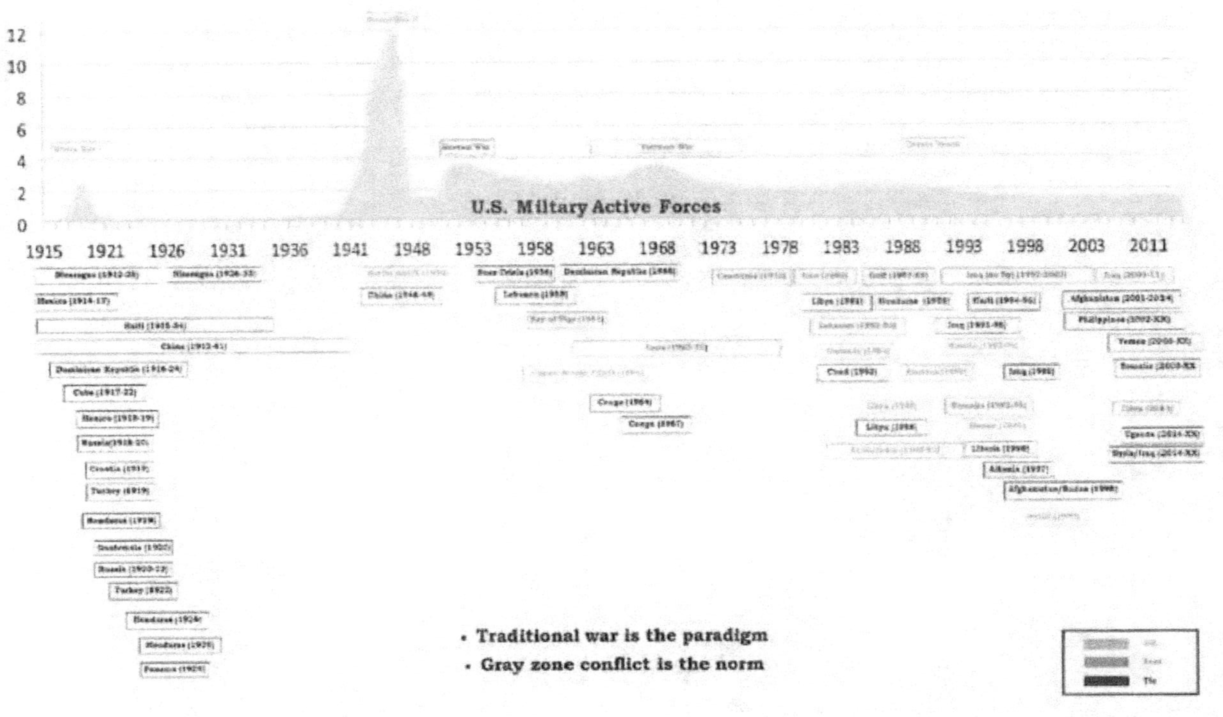

Figure 1: A century of U.S. wars, gray zone conflicts and active duty end strength

Figure 1 depicts the last 100 years of America military involvement. The U.S. military active duty end strength is shown in green, ranging from a couple hundred thousand in the early 1900's, peaking at 11 million during World War II, and gradually declining to its current strength of about 1.4 million. Above the strength graph are five conflicts during the past century fitting the traditional war model: World Wars I and II, Korea, Vietnam and Desert Storm. They feature large, force-on-force engagements by uniformed militaries fielded by nation states. Below the strength graph are 57 instances when the U.S. military conducted foreign operations.[2] The exact number can vary depending upon the criteria used to define a foreign military operation, but taken as a whole, they offer a good representation of gray zone challenges – missions falling short of a declared war, yet important enough to send American service members into harm's way. Traditional war might be the dominant paradigm of warfare, but gray zone challenges are the norm.

The last time the U.S. declared war was over seven decades ago, when President Roosevelt signed Joint Resolutions formally declaring war on Bulgaria, Hungary and Rumania on June 5th, 1942.[3] For every declared war, the U.S. military has deployed or engaged in combat scores of additional times. For example, over 40,000 U.S. troops took part in the fourteen-month invasion and occupation of the Dominican Republic to prevent it from "going Communist" in 1965-66.[4] This intervention merits little more than a footnote in American military history. The Dominican Republic foray rarely comes to mind when we discuss actions by the world's most powerful military, but it is more typical of U.S. military operations than large-scale conventional conflicts. For every traditional war the U.S. military fights, it engages in multiple gray zone operations.

Gray Zones Characteristics

Some level of *aggression* is a key determinant in shifting a challenge from the white zone of peacetime competition into the gray zone. The U.S. seeks to address disputes through diplomacy, but has always reserved the right to take military action to defend its interests, even acting upon that reservation despite multinational pressure to the contrary. We established laws, policies, authorities and mechanisms to arbitrate disagreements in peacetime, and Americans benefit greatly from an ordered world where all parties play by known rules. The post-World War II international system was established by and to the advantage of the United States and the West. A slew of state and non-state actors now aggressively oppose this Western-constructed international order, but in ways that fall short of recognized thresholds of traditional war. In simple terms, we understand war and peace and how to act during these instances, but there is a vast range of conflicts between these well-understood poles where we struggle to respond effectively.

Gray zone challenges are also *perspective-dependent*, as depicted in figure 2. In eastern Ukraine, the U.S., Russia and Ukraine interpret the conflict differently. For the U.S., the contest falls closer to the white zone, and is best handled by economic sanctions and diplomatic pressure. For Russia, it more closely approaches the black zone of war, suggesting that a willingness to act more aggressively is appropriate. Its actions emphasize the information and military lines of national power. Ukraine sees it as an existential threat to the sovereignty of its nation, justifying national

---

[2] The 57 instances were partially compiled from the Committee on Foreign Affairs and include instances when U.S. military forces were deployed overseas. They exclude instances of just military aid or CIA-only operations.
[3] Declarations of War and Authorizations for the Use of Military Force: Historical Background and Legal Implications, Jennifer Elsea and Matthew Weed, CRS, April 18th, 2014.
[4] Foreign Relations of the United States, 1964–1968 Volume XXXII, Dominican Republic; Cuba; Haiti; Guyana, U.S. Department of State, Office of the Historian.

mobilization – actions rooted deep in the black zone of potential war. Understanding the differing viewpoints of the parties involved in gray zone challenges is critical, providing insights into each party's level of commitment and how far each may be willing to go in pursuing their objectives.

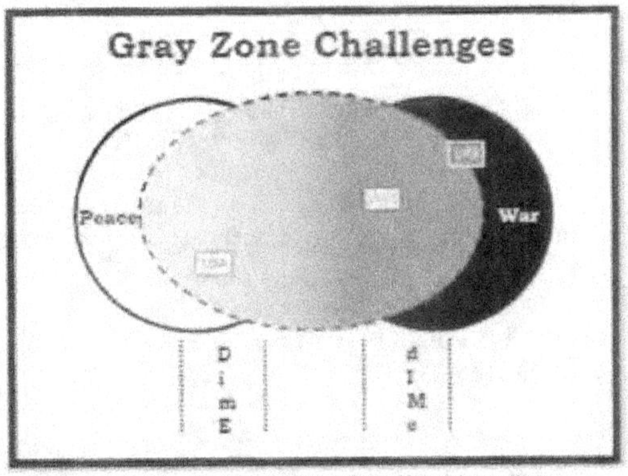

Finally, gray zone challenges feature *ambiguity* regarding the nature of the conflict, the parties involved or the relevant policy and legal frameworks. By definition, the gray zone is ambiguous, and this opaqueness results from both our own organizing principles and our adversaries' purposeful actions. We struggle when dealing with challenges not fitting neatly into our traditional models. No organization in the U.S. government has primacy for gray zone challenges, so it is unsurprising our responses lack both unity of effort and unity of command. Our adversaries are often well informed on our gray zone shortcomings, and they can act purposefully to maximize the ambiguity in a given situation. For example, Russian material and manpower assistance to separatists in the Ukraine is extensively documented, but official Russian government denials inject just enough uncertainty into the situation to blunt Western responses. The exact methods of obfuscation vary by situation, but even in the era of globalized information, adversaries can use ambiguity effectively to avoid accountability for their actions.

Figure 2: Participant perspectives of the Ukraine conflict

Gray Zones Discussed

The current international order is largely a Westphalian construct, emphasizing human rights, free-market economies, sovereignty of the nation-state, representative government and self-determination. In the past, gray zone challenges typically emanated from state-sponsored groups or nation-states adopting strategies seeking to avoid escalation. Now, non-state and proto-state organizations such as al Qaeda and Daesh (ISIS) can amass resources and connect enough formerly disparate individuals to constitute threats that cannot be ignored.

America's status as the global leader guarantees it will face multiple, constant gray zone challenges. U.S. national security interests are worldwide, and there is a set of rogue state and non-state actors defining themselves, at least in part, by standing in opposition to America and its values. The U.S. can selectively avoid some, but not all gray zone challenges. For example, the scale of Al Qaeda's 9/11 attack demanded a robust U.S. response, while the Southeast Asian terrorist group Jemaah Islamiyah's actions have not risen to the level where it is a significant concern for the U.S. national security apparatus.

Nation-states remain strong cornerstones of the international system, but the myriad challenges facing them are proliferating and strengthening faster than states' powers. Any international system maintaining a reasonable level of world order must account for numerous powerful non-state actors and multiple sources of legitimacy and governance.

The relative certainty we experienced facing the Soviet Union during the Cold War seems simpler when compared to today's disorderly global landscape. It was easier to deal with nation-states because they generally followed established rules, and these rules were typically to our advantage.

There is an elegant simplicity inherent in nation-states. They control their borders, exercise a monopoly on the legitimate use of force, and govern their populations. There is a single, centralized entity with which to negotiate, and events can proceed at the pace of diplomacy. During the Cold War, even when nation-states made deliberate choices to engage in gray zone activities, U.S. responses were still governed by the rules of state-to-state relations. This is not the case today. What differs now are the growing number of potential gray zone actors, the tools available to them, and the velocity of change. For example, it was far simpler for the State Department spokesperson to respond to the tightly controlled messages from the Soviet-era TASS than to have a ready reply for the thousands of Twitter accounts linked to Daesh (ISIS) and its supporters. The trend towards gray zone conflicts increasingly disadvantages entrenched governmental bureaucracies.

Globalization is also having a tremendous impact on gray zone challenges, and we are only beginning to understand the implications. Specifically, globalization has radically reshaped the way information flows and put technology and communications tools that were once the exclusive purview of nation-states into the hands of individuals. While it is impossible to know exactly how this mega-trend will reshape the world, it offers the potential to drive societal change on the scale of that induced by the Gutenberg printing press. The 15th century invention of movable type led to fundamental changes in language, literacy rates, the way ideas promulgated, and the very structure of society[5] – remarkably similar to what we are witnessing today. Just as Europe's literate elite had to adapt to change, so too must we evolve our current governing structures to account for a rapidly changing environment.

Nations and populations are now interconnected and interdependent in unprecedented ways. Overall, centralized government is becoming more expensive and less effective, while the tools available to non-state actors are trending the opposite way. As America experienced over the last 15 years, the price of major combat operations is escalating to the point of being cost-prohibitive. These trends portend an expanded gray zone, since nations are even more reticent to engage in open warfare, and can now find and exploit other less conventional tools of leverage. For example, European dependence on Russian energy supplies and American concerns about potential uncontrolled escalation tempered the West's response to Russia's *de facto* invasion of eastern Ukraine.

One significant challenge for the U.S is that decisive actions in the gray zone are far easier to carry out by authoritarian or centralized decision-making structures than by democratic, consensus-building governments and coalitions. Unified control of the levers of power may be anathema in democracies, but it streamlines the speed of decisions and unity of effort in the gray zone. Gray zone challenges tend to involve multiple instruments of power simultaneously, and unity of command is helpful in achieving rapid and effective results. In contrast to centralized regimes, no single person in democracies can direct all actions in the gray zone. The net effect in democracies is to create intense bureaucratic friction arising from our own organizing principles, resulting in strategic and operational rigidity. At best, we can achieve alignment of the goals and actions among our disparate countries and organizations. At worst, we experience self-induced paralysis and find ourselves constantly reacting late to more nimble autocratic gray zone actors.

---

[5] Anderson, Benedict: "Comunidades Imaginadas. Reflexiones sobre el origen y la difusión del nacionalismo", Fondo de cultura económica, Mexico 1993, ISBN 978-968-16-3867-2, pp. 63–76

In its early history, the U.S. often employed gray zone stratagems when confronting established powers. As the United States rose to become the dominant world power, this dynamic reversed. Our current national security architecture largely derives from the National Security Act of 1947, with its fundamental organizing precept focused on maintaining the world order rather than challenging it. In part because of this strategic commitment to the status quo, since World War II the U.S. has not been organized for gray zone challenges and has often not responded to them particularly well. In many ways, the United States has a yawning gap in the laws, policies, mental models, and approaches we use to deal with the gray zone. America's response to gray zone challenges tends to be either overly militarized or overly constrained. Because these challenges typically feature ambiguity in the legal and policy arenas, we cannot neatly bin the challenges as either purely peacetime or exclusively warfare. We have clear concepts and models for using law enforcement and military tools, but we struggle to apply them in the muddled middle ground.

Not every non-state actor in the gray zone deserves significant attention, and a useful benchmark for concern is when belligerent ambitions and operational reach become transnational. For example, Basque separatists in Spain and France confine their goals and actions to a relatively restricted geographic region and aspire to little more than an autonomous Basque state. In contrast, many militia groups in Libya have pledged loyalty to broader, global insurgent movements such as al Qaeda or Daesh (ISIS). These groups pose a gray zone challenge worthy of dedicated resources and action, as much for what they could become as for the danger of today. The Latin principle of *obsta principiis* (take care of bad things when they are small) applies.

Most importantly, traditional war and gray zone challenges have fundamentally divergent natures, requiring different lexicons, approaches, and executions. While they resemble each other superficially and involve the violent clash of wills, they require fundamentally different approaches. In fact, antagonists typically choose to work in the gray zone precisely because they want to avoid full-scale war and its potential to trigger an overwhelming U.S. military response. There is no universal solution to gray zone challenges, but the logic of belligerents in avoiding large-scale war remains constant. For the United States, being able to dominate one slice of the spectrum of conflict does not necessarily translate into supremacy across the full range of security challenges. We must think, plan and act differently to succeed in the gray zone.

Working in Gray Zones – Implications

America spends roughly $600 billion every year on defense, and it is the dominant global power by every objective measure. Yet state and non-state actors (e.g., Russia and Daesh (ISIS)) are increasingly undeterred from acting in ways inimical to the global common good. State actors like Russia and China reasonably believe we will not use nuclear or conventional military force to thwart their ambitions if they craft their aggressive actions to avoid clear-cut military triggers. Despite their inherent ambiguity, the United States should not be frustrated by gray zone challenges. Rather, we should aim to achieve favorable outcomes by taking some practical steps to improve our ability to address them.

Whole of Government: Our responses to gray zone challenges display several clear deficiencies. As separate U.S. government agencies strive to achieve their individual organizational goals, they seldom act in integrated ways to support wider government objectives. The National Security Act of 1947 served us well, but in an era far removed from the Cold War, the United States needs a new construct for the 21st century. There is widespread agreement that going forward, we will require an unprecedented level of Interagency (IA) coordination capable of synchronizing all elements of national power. Absent a forcing function, government organizations will simply do more of the same. The new national security structure must be responsive, integrated, and adaptable. This is a major overhaul of our security infrastructure, it will be difficult, and it will not take place overnight. The time to start is now.

We also need to grow our non-military capabilities. Our gray zone actions are often overly militarized because the Department of Defense (DOD) has the most capability and resources, and thus is often the default U.S. government answer. Having more institutional capability outside of DOD optimized to operate between the clearly defined lanes of law enforcement and full-scale war will help avoid predictable, binary U.S. responses. Our counter-Daesh (ISIS) campaign is a perfect example. Thousands of airstrikes helped to check their rapid expansion, but the decisive effort against them will require discrediting their narrative and connecting the people to legitimate governing structures – areas where DOD should not have primacy.

Root Causes: Prudent strategies recognize root causes and address them. Daesh (ISIS), for example, is merely symptomatic of the much larger problems of massive populations of disaffected Sunnis estranged from legitimate governance and a breakdown in the social order across much of Africa and the Middle East. This will only be exacerbated in coming years by worsening economic and demographic trends. Daesh (ISIS) is also a prime example of gray zone challenges, since the legal and policy framework of how to attack a proto-state is highly ambiguous. Coalition aircraft started bombing Daesh (ISIS) in August of 2014, and the authorization for the use of military force is still being debated a year later, highlighting our confusion about how to proceed. Notably, devising a realistic strategy requires a holistic understanding of the challenge and the environment. Treating gray zone challenges as war drives warfare approaches and focuses on defeating a threat. Many gray zone "threats" are really symptoms rather than being the actual "problem." As in the medical field, we should manage symptoms and cure the disease. The key is to first identify the core issue, design a strategy to focus actions, and ensure our tactical and operational activities are properly aligned. Tactical brilliance (a U.S. military strong suit) is meaningless or even counterproductive absent an overarching strategy.

Comprehensive Deterrence: Deterring emerging security challenges is far better than responding to them once a crisis erupts. Great effort went into developing deterrence theory during the Cold War, but this field languished once the Soviet Union dissolved. Deterrence in this era focused on nuclear warfare, but it suggested valuable concepts of counter-force, counter-value and countervailing targeting with potential for broader applicability, each of which is applicable to U.S. strategy in gray zone conflict. In brief, counter-value targeting aims to destroy the society, counter-force targeting aims to destroy an enemy's military capabilities, and countervailing targeting aims to deny victory by eliminating what a particular entity values. Paradoxically, each deliberate gray zone challenge represents both a success and failure of deterrence – success in averting full-scale war, but a deterrent failure given the belligerent's decision to take action in the gray zone.

Firefighting	Gray Zone Challenge
Smoke	Illegal violence
Flame	Violent extremist organizations
Accelerants	Mass communication, technology
Fuel	Identity-based populations
Heat	Ideology
Oxygen	Governance

A useful analogy is how firefighters fight fire. They do not attack the flame itself. Rather, they understand the fire triangle of fuel, heat and oxygen and tailor their actions accordingly. Similarly, we can apply fire triangle models in approaching gray zone challenges. Examining Daesh (ISIS), it is burning white hot now, but it represents only the flame. Even if all its adherents vanished tomorrow, the conditions would still exist to spawn a successor movement. Daesh (ISIS) must be dealt with, but only as part of a wider, systemic effort to address the underlying conditions allowing it to flourish.

State and non-state actors alike value identifiable people, places and things. Holding these at risk and demonstrating the will to leverage these vulnerabilities can contribute to comprehensive deterrence. Creating a credible threat of unconventional warfare aimed at countervailing targets is one possibility. For example, China is both antagonistically asserting its questionable claims to specific islands and atolls in the South China Sea while simultaneously expanding its import of raw materials from Africa. Instead of confronting China in the South China Sea directly, surrogates could theoretically be used to hold China's African interests at risk in order to compel a more favorable outcome of South China Sea disputes. Thus, the point of action (e.g., Africa) might be far removed from the point of effect (e.g., Asia), but the intent would be to alter the decision-making calculus regardless of geography. To be credible, such an approach requires prep work every bit as important as the infrastructure behind our nuclear and conventional capabilities. Capable and trustworthy surrogates are the result of years of purposeful relationship nurturing, and the vast majority of the work should take place pre-crisis.

Opportunities: A new lexicon would help us understand and engage challenges in the gray zone better. Gray zone actors purposefully seek to avoid conventional war, yet we inevitable use military terminology and planning processes to shape our response, even when there are better alternatives. Changing our terminology could also help us pursue opportunities and not just build a massive (but potentially irrelevant) defense architecture prepared for high-end armed conflict. The U.S. has the most powerful and best-equipped military in the history of the world, and it is designed to prevail in traditional wars against peer competitors with large conventional militaries. This high-end tool is often not the appropriate one to use as a main effort in the gray zone, yet we too often default to the military and its accordant vocabulary of "seizing the initiative, winning and centers of gravity," even when these are irrelevant to the particular issue at hand.

Changing our vocabulary could help yield better decisions in the gray zone. Adopting a business vocabulary and a "SWOT" model (strength, weakness, opportunity and threat) would open other opportunities not available in military decision-making models. Similar to the way businesses decide how to allocate capital, we would necessarily distinguish between opportunities and threats and have at least an estimate of our expected return on investment. Talking and thinking differently about national security in the gray zone would help us measure the oft-ignored opportunity costs and come up with some metric, however imperfect initially, to measure our expected return on investment for defense dollars.

Cost should be a significant upfront consideration. For example, we famously refused to provide a cost estimate for Operation Iraqi Freedom, other than to know that $200 billion was far too high. Assuming we established $200 billion as the top end to "invest" in Iraq, it would at least force us to review our actions and evaluate our return on investment as we blew through initial estimates on our way to spending in excess of $2 trillion.[6] Just the exercise of estimating costs and examining

---

[6] Trotta, Daniel, "Iraq war costs U.S. more than $2 Trillion: Study." Reuters, Mar 13, 2013. http://www.reuters.com/article/2013/03/14/us-iraq-war-anniversary-idUSBRE92D0PG20130314.

our actions when we reach those estimates would help frame future debates about potential interventions and their attendant opportunity costs.

Specialization. Being good at one type of conflict, say force-on-force conventional war, does not necessarily mean we are good at another type, say counterinsurgency. It would be nice if governing high-end warfare meant we were dominant across the entire gray zone, but that is not the case. War and the gray zone share some characteristics, but the fundamentally different approaches required to do both well necessitate specialization. As many senior strategists have suggested, there should be two broad categories of U.S. military forces. Category One forces should focus on conventional warfare and be powerful enough to defeat potential adversary state militaries such as North Korean. Category Two forces would focus on being able to act in the gray zone. They would feature smaller, more agile and deployable units. The two sets of forces would not necessarily be mutually exclusive, and they could support each other as needed. However, their manning, training and equipping would look quite different. The two forces would have different skill sets, orientations and day-to-day missions. As the U.S. demonstrated the ability to operate efficiently and effectively in the gray zone, it would lessen the need to do so over time. Gray zone challenges to the U.S. are increasing rapidly in the hyper-connected world of the 21st century, and having a force structure reflecting this reality is a strategic imperative.

Conclusion—Gray Can be Good

The ambiguity making gray zones so vexing also makes them useful to statesmen. In fact, they are crucial to the conduct of international relations in defining the importance of situations to the parties involved. That is, states and non-states can 'test the waters' with gray zone activities to determine the relative strength of domestic and international commitment to an endeavor without resorting to the more lethal violence of war. In brief, gray zone conflicts are an immensely better alternative to full-scale wars.

Since the end of the Cold War and subsequent triumph during Desert Storm, the United States has demonstrated it has no peer competitor in the conventional military domain. Not surprisingly, America's adversaries thus purposefully seek to avoid playing to her strengths. Precious few state and non-state actors are foolish enough to line up uniformed troops and subject them to the full wrath of American military might.

We cannot ignore gray zone challenges altogether. On the contrary, we should seek to identify, understand, and highlight activities running counter to U.S. interests. This awareness can help attribute nefarious activity, potentially increasing costs for that activity even if the U.S. does directly intervene. This understanding could also enable early application of U.S. instruments of power, ultimately operating in the gray zone to our benefit by shaping the arc of change closer to its origins. The United States already has most of the tools required to secure and advance its national security interests in the gray zone. However, it must evolve its organizational, intellectual and institutional models to flourish in the middle ground between war and peace and avoid the predictability and rigidity characterizing its actions since the end of the Cold War.

Prepared by: CAPT Philip Kapusta/USSOCOM J51/(813) 826-1717